THE
EVERYTHING®
GIANT BOOK OF JUICING

Dear Reader,

Juicing has enjoyed a phenomenal rise in popularity over the past decades, and not just among fitness freaks or gym rats. With food and produce prices on the rise, and environmental concerns about food quality making new headlines every day, it only makes sense to find ways to maximize nutrition, minimize costs, and exercise quality control right from your own kitchen.

Whether you're new to juicing or a longtime enthusiast, know that nothing beats juicing for flavor, freshness, and quality nutrition. It's fast, easy, and fun. Use the recipes I've included here and feel free to experiment by adding fresh juice to smoothies, soups, and all sorts of frozen delights. Nature provides us with a huge variety of fruits and vegetables to choose from, and you can juice them in endless combinations. So, whip up some juice, raise a glass, and make a toast: To your health!

Teresa Kennedy

Welcome to the EVERYTHING® Series!

These handy, accessible books give you all you need to tackle a difficult project, gain a new hobby, comprehend a fascinating topic, prepare for an exam, or even brush up on something you learned back in school but have since forgotten.

You can choose to read an Everything® book from cover to cover or just pick out the information you want from our four useful boxes: e-questions, e-facts, e-alerts, and e-ssentials.

We give you everything you need to know on the subject, but throw in a lot of fun stuff along the way, too.

We now have more than 400 Everything® books in print, spanning such wide-ranging categories as weddings, pregnancy, cooking, music instruction, foreign language, crafts, pets, New Age, and so much more. When you're done reading them all, you can finally say you know Everything®!

QUESTION

Answers to common questions

FACT

Important snippets of information

ALERT

Urgent warnings

ESSENTIAL

Quick handy tips

PUBLISHER Karen Cooper

MANAGING EDITOR, EVERYTHING® SERIES Lisa Laing

COPY CHIEF Casey Ebert

ASSOCIATE PRODUCTION EDITOR Mary Beth Dolan

ACQUISITIONS EDITOR Lisa Laing

SENIOR DEVELOPMENT EDITOR Brett Palana-Shanahan

EVERYTHING® SERIES COVER DESIGNER Erin Alexander

Visit the entire Everything® series at *www.everything.com*

THE EVERYTHING®
GIANT BOOK OF JUICING

Teresa Kennedy

Avon, Massachusetts

For my husband, who bravely sampled where
no juice had gone before . . .

Published by Adams Media, a division of F+W Media, Inc.
57 Littlefield Street, Avon, MA 02322. U.S.A.
www.adamsmedia.com

ISBN 10: 1-4405-5785-3
ISBN 13: 978-1-4405-5785-9
eISBN 10: 1-4405-5786-1
eISBN 13: 978-1-4405-5786-6

Printed in the United States of America.

10 9 8 7 6 5 4 3 2

Always follow safety and commonsense cooking protocol while using kitchen utensils, operating ovens and stoves, and handling uncooked food. If children are assisting in the preparation of any recipe, they should always be supervised by an adult.

Photos by Susan Whetzel.

This book is available at quantity discounts for bulk purchases.
For information, please call 1-800-289-0963.

Contents

4 Juicing for Weight Loss 79

5   Juicing for Longevity and Anti-Aging 103

7 Fast to Fabulous. 149

12   Cold Soups 239

Acknowledgments

Special thanks to Carole Jacobs and Patrice Johnson for their excellent research and recipes in the first *Everything® Juicing Book* as well as to Adams Media's editor Lisa Laing.

Introduction

IN THESE INCREASINGLY HEALTH-CONSCIOUS times, people are aware of the need for better nutrition. Concerns over pesticides, genetic engineering, the empty calories, added sugars, and trans fats in commercially prepared convenience foods all make headlines as authorities try to teach the need for better nutrition.

A good diet is key to good health. Yet, despite a myriad of movements toward whole foods and health foods, the typical American diet tends to fall a bit short of the mark. Crazy schedules, busy lifestyles, and increased dependence on convenience foods have taken us a long way from the days where backyard gardens flourished and everything that came out of the kitchen was made from scratch. Too, there's a bewildering array of advice out there as to what to include and what to avoid in your daily diet as a means of maintaining good health. But the fact remains, everyone agrees that including greater amounts of fresh fruits and vegetables is essential. Experts recommend anywhere from five to nine servings of fruits and vegetables every day.

Realistically though, that's easier said than done. Even the best dietary intentions can fall by the wayside when faced with finicky kids, rising grocery prices, and the ever-present temptation of added convenience. Things get even more confusing with the seemingly never-ending array of information about foods that are "bad" for you.

The good news is that regular juicing provides a great answer for those who want a better balance in their diets with a minimum investment in time, money, and effort. Juicing is something you can add to your daily routine without necessarily having to give up the foods you enjoy or spending endless hours in the kitchen. It requires almost nothing by way of preparation, and is faster and easier than popping something in the microwave. Best of all, you can be confident in the knowledge that just by juicing three to four times a week, you and your family will gain maximum nutrition, an increase in overall good health and immunity, and all the antioxidant and disease-fighting benefits you need to thrive.

Why fresh juice? Because juicing extracts essential nutrients and vitamins by breaking down fruits and vegetables at the cellular level. The resulting "liquid nutrition" is absorbed into the body almost instantaneously and far more efficiently than by popping a multivitamin. Unlike prepackaged or prepared juices, fresh juice isn't pasteurized, as required by the FDA. Although pasteurizing is meant to be a protection, the heating process can destroy much of the original nutritional value. The logic is simple: Whole, living foods provide the best nutrition for living beings. Fresh juice is pure quality, provides instant bio-availability and immediate and tangible rewards.

As science uncovers more and more information about the benefits of juicing, people have come to understand that many of the micronutrients, phytochemicals, and enzymes available in whole, raw fruits and vegetables simply aren't available when those same foods are eaten raw or cooked. This is because they are not absorbed or digested in the same way that fresh juices are.

What are some of these nutrients? Amino acids, which form the building blocks for protein; soluble fiber that helps control bad cholesterol; essential fatty acids that the body cannot make on its own, yet which are essential to healthy nerve cells and form part of the cellular membrane around all cells; phytochemicals that give plants their unique colors, tastes, and scents, and which have antioxidant and anti-carcinogenic properties. Minerals, such as calcium, potassium, iron, and zinc, that are essential to proper cell functioning. Enzymes, which aid in digestion and regulate chemical reactions in the body, and, last but not least—vitamins, vitamins, vitamins! Fruit and vegetable juices contain vitamins A, C, D, E, and K, as well as B-complex vitamins, all essential to maintaining good health.

Though many people first come to juicing seeking help for a specific ailment or condition, there's no need to wait for something to go wrong before you try it! The human body has a remarkable capacity to fight disease, to heal, and even to renew itself. When you give it the nutrients it needs, it will respond in amazing ways, rewarding you by regulating your weight, increasing your levels of energy, fighting the effects of time, and even reducing your need to conventionally medicate conditions such as high blood pressure, metabolism, and even acne! The cleansing power of juice makes it clear that the body knows what it's doing. Adding the good stuff helps get rid of the bad. That's a "health insurance plan" nobody can afford to turn down.

CHAPTER 1

The Juicing Evolution

A lot of people like to talk about the so-called juicing revolution, but the fact is, juicing has been around for a long, long time. In a way, we're not so much discovering the health benefits of consuming greater amounts of fruits and vegetables as we're rediscovering them. Back when family farms were the norm rather than the exception, people ate well because they ate what they grew. Today's movements for sustainability, reduced use of pesticides and fertilizers, and relying more on local food supplies have all revealed the wisdom of a better diet.

At the same time, modern technology makes juicing accessible to more people than ever before. When fresh produce meets a modern juicer, it constitutes a true evolution in the way we think about nutrition. It's fast, easy, delicious, and good for you, too!

History

Juicing has been around for centuries, playing a large role in healing and medicine. The Dead Sea Scrolls contain several references for the preparation of medicinal juices, and the ancient Indian tradition of Ayurvedic medicine utilized ingredients such as limes, oranges, grapes, beets, radishes, and mango.

The modern age of juicing began in the early 1930s when difficult economic times made consumers think harder about ways to stay healthy and maximize the nutritional value of foods. The first modern juicer was created by a man named Dr. Norman Walker, who must have been well aware of the benefits of the practice, because he lived to be 108 years old! After World War II, the advent of technology came to the kitchen along with such dubious improvements as TV dinners and commercially canned products, and there was less of an emphasis on healthy eating habits. But in the 1960s, the publication of books such as *Diet for a Small Planet* sparked renewed consumer interest in organic and health-conscious eating.

ESSENTIAL

Local foods have replaced organic foods as the most dynamic sector of the retail food market. Sales of local foods grew from $4 billion in 2002 to $5 billion in 2007 and were more than $11 billion in 2011. Organic food sales still exceed $20 billion per year, but the rate of growth in organic food sales seems to be slowing even as local food sales are accelerating. For many people, *local* has become more important than *organic*.

In the 1970s, Linus Pauling, two-time winner of the Nobel Prize, brought the importance of daily doses of vitamin C to public attention and its importance in fighting disease and ailments such as the common cold. In his book, *How to Live Longer and Feel Better*, Dr. Pauling reviewed an enormous amount of scientific literature to discover and demonstrate that large doses of real vitamins and minerals do cure real diseases. A pioneer in American allopathic medicine, he emphasized the role of proper nutrition and vitamins in maintaining health.

Today, modern FDA guidelines mandate four to five servings of vegetables and fruits per day. Modern foodies are embracing healthier living concurrent with a rise in concern over how commercially produced foods may be contaminated by a variety of environmental factors and farming practices. Going organic and buying local are both on the rise and these factors have, in turn, led to a renewed interest in how to get the most nutritional bang for your food buck and maintain optimum health at the same time.

Going Raw

Many food experts maintain that raw foods are the healthiest for the body, because heating foods above 110 degrees is thought to denature enzymes that are naturally present. Those enzymes are thought to be the life force of foods, helping the body to digest and absorb nutrients. In some cases that's certainly true. Vitamin C, for example is destroyed by heat, and the cancer-fighting sulforaphanes found in broccoli are diminished by heating.

FACT

Consuming raw foods as a health treatment was first developed in Switzerland by a medical doctor, Maximilian Bircher-Benner, who was also the inventor of muesli. After recovering from jaundice while eating raw apples, he conducted a variety of experiments into the effects of raw vegetables on human health. In 1897, he opened a sanatorium in Zurich called "Vital Force," named after a "key term from the German lifestyle reform movement which states that people should pattern their lives after the logic determined by nature." It is still treating patients today.

In other cases, though, cooking can actually increase nutritional value. The lycopenes in tomatoes, for example, increase when the fruit is cooked, but that's because the fibrous portions are broken down. Kale, garlic, spinach, and onions have also been shown to be more nutritious cooked as light cooking releases compounds that might otherwise go undigested. Whether or not you're a raw foods advocate, it's important to do your homework, and, as always, balance is the key in any diet.

Whatever your food choices, regular juicing offers the best of both worlds. First, because you gain all the benefits of raw foods, and second, because juicing breaks down the fibrous portions of fruits and vegetables at the cellular level to maximize their nutritive value. More than any other dietary practice, juicing puts the "whole" back in whole foods and offers great economy, digestibility, and nutrition without a huge adjustment in lifestyle.

Juicing Versus Blending

While it's true that a good high-speed blender can give you many of the same benefits as juicing, blending doesn't break down fibers of fruits and vegetables at the cellular level. Thus, you may not derive the same nutritional punch as with a juicer. Still, a good high-quality blender can be useful in concocting smoothies, soups, and frozen treats with your fresh juices, so they're good to have around.

Some newer technology claims to have narrowed the gap between juicers and blenders with higher speeds and greater cellular breakdown, especially in "bullet" type machines, but it's important to keep in mind that even the best blender will result in liquids with greater amounts of pulp and fiber, which may be harder to digest and absorb than juice products. Some juicing proponents claim that higher speeds and the resulting heat from powerful motors destroy valuable nutrients, but so far, there's not a lot of evidence to support that claim. If any machine is running so hot that it's heating your juice, it's best to put it in retirement and look for something new.

Fresh Is Best

Unless you're growing your own, it's often difficult to determine where produce comes from or how long it's been in your supermarket aisle. If you're someone concerned about food pedigree, be sure to check for labels. Often they're an indicator if the produce was grown outside the United States or in a country where laws governing the use of pesticides or chemical fertilizers aren't as stringent as they are here.

Local farmers' markets are a great source for fresh produce as are food cooperatives. Food "rescue" organizations are also springing up all over the country, purchasing fresh produce in bulk from farmers, restaurant, and grocery chains and selling them to members at significantly reduced prices. Members report that for a contribution of as little as ten dollars they can receive up to sixty pounds of fresh produce.

FACT

The more vibrant the color, the more powerful the juice. Flavonoids are the plant pigments responsible for the colors in fruits and vegetables. But they also have anti-allergic, ant-inflammatory, anti-carcinogenic, and antiviral properties. What pleases the eye is also likely to please the palate, so drink up!

When shopping for and selecting the best produce for your juicer, a good rule to follow is the G-R-O-W rule (greens, reds, oranges, and whites). It's perhaps not such a coincidence that the fruits and veggies with the most eye appeal and the deepest, most vivid colors are also likely to be the most nutritious. Greens include lettuces, spinach, broccoli, Swiss chard, and kale. Reds include beets, red cabbage, raspberries, strawberries, and red peppers. The orange group includes carrots, sweet potatoes, cantaloupe, oranges, and pumpkins. Last but not least, the "w" stands for white—cabbage, parsnips, and cauliflower.

Storage

Whether it's organic, nonorganic, or so fresh you picked it off the tree yourself, always wash your fruits and vegetables before you juice. Store your produce in the refrigerator whenever possible, and if you have a humidity setting in your vegetable drawer, keep it on the high side in dryer, more arid zones such as Arizona, parts of California, Utah, and other Western states, as higher humidity makes for longer keeping, If you live in a moister environment such as the Pacific Northwest, or along the eastern seaboard, lower humidity settings are appropriate. The more water content the produce has, the greater the yield of juice. Most produce for juicing can be safely kept for a week or more in the refrigerator, depending on what it is. Lettuces and leafy greens like spinach will begin to deteriorate after a week, but root vegetables like carrots or beets will keep much longer. And while it may seem obvious to point it out, any bruises, spots, or blemishes should be trimmed away before juicing. Pick over berries and discard any that may have become overripe or wrinkled.

The Organic Controversy

An "organic" label doesn't necessarily guarantee consumer quality. Because the movement has become so popular, many companies have jumped on the bandwagon. Whether or not you choose organic, do know some fruits and vegetables are more susceptible to absorbing chemicals and pesticides than others.

Even if you do choose organic produce, be especially aware that there are some fruits and veggies that are more susceptible to environmental factors than others. E. coli, for example, occurs naturally, as does anthrax, even under organically raised conditions. So rinse, rinse, rinse before juicing.

The Environmental Working Group, which, among other things, analyzes produce and identifies susceptibility to pesticide and chemical residue, has identified the "Dirty Dozen" and stresses the importance of buying them from a reliable organic source. They are:

- Apples
- Celery
- Sweet bell peppers
- Peaches
- Strawberries
- Nectarines
- Grapes
- Spinach
- Lettuce
- Cucumbers
- Blueberries
- Potatoes

Their list of fruits and veggies where an organic label might not be so important includes:

- Onions
- Corn
- Pineapple
- Avocado
- Cabbage
- Sweet peas
- Asparagus
- Mangoes
- Eggplant
- Kiwi
- Cantaloupe
- Grapefruit

Whatever your choice, do know that many companies and producers are hopping on the organic bandwagon. So check your labels carefully. There's a difference between a "certified" organic label and a "transitional" organic label. The "transitional" label means that the grower may have used pesticides and chemicals in the past and, while they have applied for certification, may not get it.

In the best of all possible worlds, of course, you have your own garden and can exercise quality control from your own backyard. For those fortunate enough to have a garden or orchard, juicing is a great way to utilize excess yields without resorting to canning or sugar-laden preserving methods. Best of all, leftover pulp from your juicers makes excellent compost material, and you can return the gift back to the soil that produced it.

To Peel or Not to Peel?

The best guide to deciding which fruits and vegetables should be peeled or cored before juicing is your own common sense. You wouldn't, for example, eat an unpeeled orange, so chances are that orange peel isn't going to make for great juice, either. Same holds true for the majority of citrus fruits. When you eat an apple, a pear, or a mango, you throw away the core, don't you? So there's no need to include it. On the other hand, you can lose significant amounts of nutrients should you peel a cucumber before juicing. Those peels are rich in chlorophyll and provide a significant amount of vitamins. If the cucumber has been waxed though, it's better peeled.

ESSENTIAL

If you're using a centrifugal style juicer, it's a good idea to juice denser fruits and vegetables like carrots, sweet potatoes, and beets first, followed by softer, juicier fruits and veggies. Denser produce will pass more easily through the clean shredding filter, and the juicier produce will help to "rinse" it to avoid clogs!

Some other peels do more harm than good, no matter what their nutritive value. Consider that including the peel of a yam or sweet potato may add nutrients, but they won't be much help if the resulting juice tastes like dirt! Perhaps the best advice though is to consider the power and the efficiency of the juicer itself and respect your equipment. Don't feed it more than it can comfortably handle. The extra teaspoon of juice you get from including a core is harder on the machine. Woody stems on broccoli or asparagus should definitely be removed. They may damage the machine, and they don't contain much juice anyhow! So use your head, use your palate, and let your senses be your guide. You'll be a master juicer in no time.

Which Juicer Is Right for You?

With the wealth of information available to you through the Internet, television advertising, and other sources, people interested in juicing are faced with what can seem like a bewildering array of choices when it comes to the "best" juicers out there. While it's important to do your homework before investing in any kitchen appliance, it's also important to keep in mind that most of the information is designed to get you to choose one product over another. We've simplified the process by identifying the three basic types of juicers and the benefits (and drawbacks) of each. But whatever you choose, remember, the best juicer is always the one that fits your needs.

Centrifugal Juicers

Centrifugal juicers are by far the most popular because of their low-to-moderate pricing and can be the right choice if you're new to juicing. Using a simple design, they operate by a spinning basket that shreds the produce and forces the juice through a strainer while the pulp is usually ejected into a container. The process adds oxygen to the juice and some models can produce a fair amount of froth or foam. Many of the newer machines come with celebrity endorsements and some attractive high-tech features. But at the low end, they can be loud, difficult to clean, and without enough power to handle the demands of a two-week juice fast. Of particular note is a tendency to "walk" during operation, making some models hazardous for kids and even some adults to operate. After all, you don't want fresh juice all over the kitchen floor!

Some juice enthusiasts maintain that the higher speeds of centrifugal models can lead to oxidation and destruction of phytochemicals and enzymes through overheating, but it's doubtful than any machine will heat the juice to the point where it loses significant nutritional value. High speeds do produce more foam though, so be sure to mix your juice thoroughly before drinking it.

Masticating Juicers

Single-gear or "masticating" juicers are more expensive, but their slower process delivers higher-quality nutrition. Using a "cold press" method, juicers compress fruit and vegetables to "squeeze" out their juice. Rugged and long lasting, they are also terrific for creating healthy kitchen concoctions like gourmet nut butters, pestos, mustards, herb blends, and other delights. They can be quite heavy, however, and the less compact models take up a fair amount of real estate on your countertop. So if you're short on space or ready outlet access, consider one of the more "portable" models.

Triturating Juicers

Double-gear or "triturating" machines tend to be the most expensive, and proponents insist they deliver the highest-quality juice. Twin-gear triturating juicers are built to provide you the best in terms of yield and nutrition.

The twin or dual gears slowly draw the produce into and through the gears, breaking down the produce into a mega dose of nutrition-packed juice. Perhaps the greatest recommendation is that they don't just make juice. They can also make salsas, ice creams, and even baby food. Their slower process takes more time, and in some models, cleanup can be more complicated. Still, they remain the optimum choice for hard-core juice aficionados due to the superior efficiency at juicing things such as wheatgrass and sprouts.

FACT

The size of the feed tube in a juicer is usually an excellent indicator of the machine's overall efficiency. Some models have smaller feed tubes to ensure that fruits and veggies are fed into the machine at slower speed. Though slower speeds tend to be favored in terms of nutrition, a small feed tube adds to preparation time and can be an indicator of a less powerful motor.

Ultimately, your choice of juicers depends on a number of factors—budget, space, time, ease, and efficiency of operation and cleaning. Do look for a juicer with multiple speeds, an adequately sized feed tube so you don't waste time prechopping, and for a machine with at least 400 watts of power to start.

Where to Buy Juicers

Whatever variety of juicer you choose, most models are widely available through large retailers such as Macy's, Walmart, and Best Buy. Online outlets such as Overstock.com can also be a good shopping source. Expect to pay between $50 and $300 for a quality machine at retail. Some of the most recommended models are the Breville Juice Fountain Elite 800JEXL, Hamilton Beach Big Mouth Pro 67650, The Green Star GS 2000, The Jack LaLanne Power Juicer Pro E-1189, and the Omega 4000. Consider any brand that has served you well in other appliances like food processors, blenders, and the like. Black & Decker, for example, launched its line of small kitchen appliances only after decades of manufacturing power tools. While they may not be top of the line, the motors are rugged and reliable.

Budget-minded? You might also consider a used model. A juicer, like so many small kitchen appliances, is one of those things people either use regularly or they don't. So it's not unusual to come across a "still in the box" model at your local thrift store, or a store return up for auction on eBay. Bargain hunters can find some great values, but just make sure these "second-hand" machines are clean and in good condition before you buy.

CHAPTER 2

The Super Juices

Nutrition experts have identified some important "superfoods" that they believe you need to maintain your good health and even kick it up a notch or two. These foods have a multitude of benefits; they can help prevent diseases such as cancer, diabetes, high cholesterol, and high blood pressure, but they can also have some equally welcome effects such as lightening mood and increased energy. To make the list, a food must have extraordinarily high levels of vitamins and other nutrients. Best of all, the list of superfoods includes a big variety of fruits and vegetables that are perfect for juicing!

What Are the Superfoods?

According to the Mayo Clinic, the following foods are on the superfoods list:

- Apples
- Avocado
- Beans
- Blueberries
- Broccoli
- Garlic
- Honey
- Kiwi
- Onions
- Oranges
- Pomegranates
- Pumpkin
- Spinach
- Tomatoes

Although the list of superfoods includes additional things, like dark chocolate, oats, and salmon, for purposes of juicing, these are the most important fruits and veggies to consider as you embark on a juicing plan. Additional research indicates that kale, cabbage, and greens such as collards and mustard greens also pack a real nutritional punch. Point is, each and every one of these foods is low in calories, high in nutrients, and offers a powerhouse of health benefits. All of them are simple, wholesome, living foods and a welcome addition to anyone's diet.

FACT

The term "superfood" was first referenced by Aaron Moss in the journal *Nature Nutrition* in 1998. He stated that: "Humans have many options when it comes to fueling their bodies, but the benefits of some options are so nutritious that they might be labeled as superfoods." Since then, the term has been co-opted by a variety of marketing organizations. As of July 2007, the marketing of products as "superfoods" is prohibited in the European Union unless accompanied by a specific medical claim supported by credible scientific research.

Going for the Green

Green vegetables are readily available and highly nutritious, but most people just don't eat enough of them. Studies continuously confirm that those who have a diet high in green leafies run a far lower risk of diseases such as heart disease and cancer. One of the reasons greens are so highly favored is because they contain high doses of chlorophyll, easily digestible proteins, enzymes, and a wide range of vitamins and minerals. These vegetables act like a mini-transfusion for the blood and a tonic for the brain, in addition to pumping up the immune system. Good choices for juicing include arugula or rocket, spinach, dandelion greens, kale, watercress, parsley, lettuce, and broccoli rabe.

Surprising Sprouts

One reason health experts favor sprouts is because, surprisingly enough, most sprouts contain highly concentrated nutrition, often far more than the mature vegetable. Sprouts do little to change the flavor of juice, but adding a handful of alfalfa, broccoli, or bean sprouts to your juices can add significant nutrition. Two powerhouses of the sprout family are wheatgrass and barley grass. Wheatgrass, or the sprouted grass of a wheatseed, don't contain the gluten or other allergens commonly associated with wheat and is wonderful for healthy blood. It also normalizes the thyroid gland and stimulates metabolism (especially for postmenopausal women) and is thought to prevent buildup of the dreaded "belly fat" as well as promoting overall weight loss.

Barley is one of the most nutrient-packed grains available, so it only makes sense that barley sprouts, or barley grass, is one of the sprout superstars. Barley grass has ten times more calcium than milk, six times more iron than spinach, and more vitamin C than orange juice. These sprouts also contain significant amounts of vitamin B_{12}. Barley grass juice has antiviral activities and neutralizes heavy metals such as mercury in the blood.

Superfood Juices

Blueberry Blast

Food scientists agree that blueberries are packed with antioxidants, phytoflavinoids, potassium, and vitamin C. Not only can they lower your risk of heart disease and cancer, they are also anti-inflammatory. Many doctors believe inflammation is the underlying cause for many diseases, so it only makes sense to stop them before they start!

INGREDIENTS | YIELDS 1½ CUPS

1 cup blueberries
2 large carrots, trimmed
½ cup fresh pineapple chunks

Out of Season?

Are blueberries not in season where you live? Not a problem. Frozen blueberries pack the same nutritional punch as fresh.

1. Following the manufacturer's instructions, process the blueberries, carrots, and pineapple in any order you wish.

2. Stir or shake the juice to blend completely, adding ice as desired.

3. Drink as soon as possible after blending.

PER SERVING: Calories: 184 | Fat: 1g | Protein: 3g | Sodium: 101mg | Carbohydrates: 46g | Sugar: 29g

Orange Strawberry Banana Juice

Yum! Once you've made it yourself, you'll find there's just no comparison to the store-bought brand.

INGREDIENTS | YIELDS 1½ CUPS

1 large orange, peeled
1 cup strawberries
1 banana, peeled

1. Process the orange and the strawberries through an electronic juicer according to the manufacturer's directions.

2. Add the banana and transfer to a blender until the mixture is smooth. Serve immediately.

PER SERVING: Calories: 237 | Fat: 1g | Protein: 4g | Sodium: 2mg | Carbohydrates: 59g | Sugar: 38g

Boost Juice

It's too bad that so many people are relying on so-called energy drinks when the juice alternative is so much healthier! Try this the next time you need a boost.

INGREDIENTS | YIELDS 1½ CUPS

1 small sweet potato, peeled
1 large carrot, trimmed
2 ripe pears, cored
3 medium oranges, peeled

Pears for Good Health

A great flavor complement and sweetener for many juices, pears are also rich in vitamins B_1 and B_2 and are considered by food experts to be hypoallergenic. When juicing pears, choose harder varieties, such as Bosch or Anjou. Softer pears yield less juice and more pulp to your mixture.

1. Wash fruits and vegetables thoroughly. Cut the sweet potato into pieces.

2. Process the carrot and sweet potato through your juicer according to manufacturer's directions.

3. Add the pears and orange segments and process.

4. Mix the juice thoroughly before serving.

PER SERVING: Calories: 383 | Fat: 1g | Protein: 5g | Sodium: 73mg | Carbohydrates: 97g | Sugar: 61g

Spicy Cucumber

*Cucumbers are rich in chlorophyll and silica.
They are a natural diuretic and benefit the digestion.*

INGREDIENTS | YIELDS 1 CUP

1 cucumber
1 clove garlic, peeled
2 green onions, trimmed
½ jalapeño pepper
2 small key limes or Mexican limes

1. Process the ingredients in any order through an electronic juicer according to the manufacturer's directions.

2. Stir to mix the juice and serve over ice.

PER SERVING: Calories: 98 | Fat: 1g | Protein: 3.5g | Sodium: 12mg | Carbohydrates: 27g | Sugar: 9g

Bean Machine

Any variety of green beans will do for this recipe, but the flat, Roma variety does yield more juice.

INGREDIENTS | YIELDS 1 CUP

2 cups fresh green beans
5 large leaves romaine lettuce
1 cucumber
1 lemon cut into quarters, peeled

Green Bean Facts

Green beans provide a good source of protein, thiamin, riboflavin, niacin, vitamin B$_6$, calcium, iron, magnesium, phosphorus, potassium, and copper.

1. Process the beans through your electronic juicer according to the manufacturer's directions.

2. Add the lettuce, followed by the cucumber and the lemon.

3. Mix the juice thoroughly to combine the ingredients and serve alone or over ice.

PER SERVING: Calories: 137 | Fat: 1g | Protein: 8g | Sodium: 30mg | Carbohydrates: 30g | Sugar: 13g

Power Punch

Punch up your energy levels with this sharp and citrusy potion.

INGREDIENTS | YIELDS 1½ CUPS

1 medium yam, peeled
4 medium oranges, peeled
2 medium carrots, trimmed
½ fresh pineapple, peeled and cut into chunks

1. Cut the yam into pieces as required. Process through your electronic juicer according to the manufacturer's directions.

2. Add the orange segments, a few at a time.

3. Add the carrots and pineapple chunks.

4. Mix resulting juice thoroughly before serving.

PER SERVING: Calories: 497 | Fat: 1.5g | Protein: 9g | Sodium: 113mg | Carbohydrates: 129g | Sugar: 77g

Vegetable Super Juice

*Add a generous dash of hot sauce to this juice for extra zip!
It's great on the rocks for a fast summer lunch.*

INGREDIENTS | YIELDS 1½ CUPS

1 whole cucumber
6 leaves romaine lettuce
4 stalks of celery, including leaves
2 cups fresh spinach
½ cup alfalfa sprouts
½ cup fresh parsley

Sandy Spinach?

Spinach grows best in sandy soils, but can be tough to really rinse well. Rather than rinsing spinach through a colander, place it in a deep bowl or kettle and cover it with water. Gently toss to allow any sand or grit to fall to the bottom and lift the greens out.

1. Cut the cucumber into pieces and process through your juicer according to the manufacturer's directions.

2. Wrap the lettuce leaves around the celery stalks and add to the feeding tube.

3. Add the spinach, sprouts, and parsley in any order you desire.

4. Mix the juice thoroughly before serving.

PER SERVING: Calories: 127 | Fat: 1.5g | Protein: 8g | Sodium: 212mg | Carbohydrates: 25g | Sugar: 10g

Vampire Chaser

*Not only does garlic chase away vampires and werewolves, it's wonderful for your health.
No worries though, the parsley will counteract any bad breath.*

INGREDIENTS | YIELDS 1½ CUPS

1 large cucumber
2 cloves garlic, peeled
½ cup parsley

1. Process the cucumber, garlic, and parsley through an electronic juicer according to the manufacturer's directions.

2. Serve the juice alone or over ice.

PER SERVING: Calories: 32 | Fat: 0.3g | Protein: 1.8g | Sodium: 19mg | Carbohydrates: 7g | Sugar: 1.5g

The Beet Master

Author Tom Robbins once described the beet as "the world's most serious vegetable." When it comes to all-around good health, increased energy, and healing powers, he might well have been right! Beet juice cleanses the liver and kidneys, helps lower blood pressure, and also helps to replenish the body's red blood cells.

INGREDIENTS | YIELDS 1 CUP

2 medium beets
2 apples, cored
1 medium orange, peeled
2 stalks celery, with leaves

Sweeten It Up!

For best juicing results use sugar beets, a hybrid beet that is sweeter than other varieties. Even at their best, however, beets can have an earthy flavor, and so are best combined with apples or carrots for a tastier juice.

1. Scrub and trim the beets. Cut into chunks.

2. Process beet chunks through the feed tube of an electronic juicer according to the manufacturer's directions.

3. Cut the apples into chunks and add to the juicer, along with the orange and the celery.

4. Mix the juice thoroughly and serve over ice.

PER SERVING: Calories: 283 | Fat: 1g | Protein: 5g | Sodium: 191mg | Carbohydrates: 70g | Sugar: 54g

Blueberry Apple

If you prefer, you can add spring water or serve over ice to dilute this one a bit.

INGREDIENTS | YIELDS 1 CUP

2 cups fresh or frozen blueberries
1 apple, cored
1 wedge lemon or lime, peeled

1. Process the berries through your electronic juicer according to the manufacturer's directions.

2. Add the apple, followed by the lemon or lime.

3. Stir or shake the juice thoroughly to combine the ingredients and serve.

PER SERVING: Calories: 248 | Fat: 1.2g | Protein: 2.7g | Sodium: 3mg | Carbohydrates: 64g | Sugar: 45g

The Energizer

Need a jolt?
This concoction will perk you up and keep you on your toes.

INGREDIENTS | YIELDS 2 CUPS

2 apples, cored
½ cucumber
¼ bulb fennel
3 stalks celery, including leaves
½ lemon, peeled
1 piece ginger, about ¼ inch
½ cup kale
½ cup spinach
6 leaves romaine lettuce

Balance the Flavor

Adding citrus, apples, and ginger to predominantly green juices brightens the flavor to offset the sometimes bitter taste of greens such as kale.

1. Slice the apples and process through the feed tube of an electronic juicer according to the manufacturer's directions.

2. Follow with pieces of cucumber and fennel.

3. Add the celery, followed by the lemon and the ginger.

4. Lightly tear the remaining greens into pieces and process.

5. Mix the juice thoroughly before serving. Serve over ice if desired.

PER SERVING: Calories: 277 | Fat: 1.8g | Protein: 7.5g | Sodium: 170mg | Carbohydrates: 67g | Sugar: 40g

Mean Green Machine

*Got a full day ahead? This one will make sure
you get through it with energy to spare.*

INGREDIENTS | YIELDS 2½ CUPS

1 cup fresh pineapple, peeled and
chopped

1 medium Granny Smith apple, cored

2 cups baby spinach leaves

¼ cup parsley

2 tablespoons mint leaves

½ pink grapefruit, peeled and seeded

1 cup coconut water

Coconut Water

Inside the humble coconut is a tropical
elixir that's packed with a unique compound of simple sugars, vitamins, minerals,
electrolytes, enzymes, amino acids, and
more. The benefits associated with coconut
water are believed to be good for the
heart, anti-aging, and anti-carcinogenic.
Use fresh or canned coconut water in your
juice recipes depending on availability.

1. Process the pineapple chunks in an electronic juicer according to the manufacturer's directions.

2. Slice the apple and add pieces to the juicer, maintaining the juicer speed.

3. Wash the spinach, parsley, and mint. Add to the juicer.

4. Add the grapefruit segments.

5. Whisk the juice together with the coconut water until well blended. Chill or serve immediately over ice.

PER SERVING: Calories: 246 | Fat: 1g | Protein: 5g |
Sodium: 70mg | Carbohydrates: 61g | Sugar: 44g

Super Sprout

Using sprouts in your juice recipes has some great advantages. First, sprouts are milder in flavor, so if you don't like radishes, you can use radish sprouts instead, as sprouts don't significantly change the flavor of any of your juices. Further, most sprouts contain much higher concentrations of micronutrients than the mature vegetable and are an easy way to pack your juice with an extra healthy punch.

INGREDIENTS | YIELDS 1 CUP

½ cup broccoli sprouts
½ cup bean sprouts
½ cup alfalfa sprouts
3 medium carrots, trimmed
1 medium apple, cored
1 medium orange, peeled

1. Process the sprouts through the feed tube of an electronic juicer according to the manufacturer's directions.

2. Add the carrots, one at a time, maintaining speed.

3. Cut the apple into chunks and add.

4. Add the orange segments.

5. Mix the juice thoroughly before serving.

PER SERVING: Calories: 211 | Fat: 1.5g | Protein: 8.2g | Sodium: 170mg | Carbohydrates: 48g | Sugar: 27g

Lettuce Play

Some say lettuce has a sedative effect, so this makes a good nightcap.

INGREDIENTS | YIELDS 1½ CUPS

½ head romaine lettuce
½ head red leaf lettuce
2 sticks celery, with leaves

1. Process the lettuces and celery through an electronic juicer according to the manufacturer's directions.

2. Serve the juice alone or over ice.

PER SERVING: Calories: 80 | Fat: 1g | Protein: 6g | Sodium: 75mg | Carbohydrates: 15g | Sugar: 5g

Best of Both Worlds

*Some of the best fruits are combined with the best veggies
in a winning combination for maximum benefit.*

INGREDIENTS | YIELDS 1½ CUPS

4–6 medium carrots, trimmed
1 medium sweet potato, peeled
1 red bell pepper, seeded
2 kiwis
1 (1-inch) piece ginger
½ lemon, peeled
2 stalks celery, with leaves

1. Process the carrots through an electronic juicer according to the manufacturer's directions.

2. Add the sweet potato, followed by the pepper.

3. Add the kiwis and the ginger.

4. Add the lemon and the celery.

5. Whisk or shake the juice thoroughly to combine and serve alone or over ice.

PER SERVING: Calories: 386 | Fat: 2g | Protein: 8.5g | Sodium: 347mg | Carbohydrates: 89g | Sugar: 26g

Simple Pleasure

If you had to pick one juice to incorporate regularly into your diet for its all-around health benefits, this one should be it. Simple and delicious.

INGREDIENTS | YIELDS 1 CUP

4 large carrots, trimmed
1 orange, peeled

1. Process the carrots through an electronic juicer according to the manufacturer's directions.

2. Add the orange segments.

3. Whisk or shake the juice to combine, and serve.

PER SERVING: Calories: 179 | Fat: 1g | Protein: 4g | Sodium: 198mg | Carbohydrates: 42g | Sugar: 25g

Red, White, and Black

Commercial cultivation of black currants was once banned by many states in the United States because the bushes can carry a fungus that is lethal for many pine trees. But in 2001, those bans began to be lifted, bringing these highly nutritious berries back on the market.

INGREDIENTS | YIELDS 1½ CUPS

1 cup red grapes
1 cup white grapes
½ cup black currants

Black Currants

Studies have shown black currants have potential benefits against cancer, aging, inflammation, and neurological diseases.

1. Process the grapes through an electronic juicer according to the manufacturer's directions.

2. Add the currants.

3. Serve the juice alone or over ice.

PER SERVING: Calories: 243 | Fat: 1g | Protein: 3g | Sodium: 7mg | Carbohydrates: 63g | Sugar: 46g

Pineapple Celery Cocktail

Pineapple is not only rich in vitamin C, it contains powerful anti-inflammatory ingredients. That, coupled with celery's excellent hydration, make this an ideal après workout treat.

INGREDIENTS | YIELDS 1 CUP

3 (1-inch) slices fresh pineapple, peeled
3 stalks celery, with leaves

More Than Meets the Eye

Although celery doesn't seem like a super-food, its health benefits are almost too lengthy to describe. The effects of celery on the body are diuretic, expectorant, carminative, anti-asthmatic, and it also aids in digestion, lowers blood pressure, is calmative, and is believed to strengthen a weak sex drive.

1. Process the pineapple chunks and celery through your juicer.

2. Serve the juice immediately.

PER SERVING: Calories: 145 | Fat: 0.5g | Protein: 2g | Sodium: 98mg | Carbohydrates: 36g | Sugar: 27g

Cucumber Honeydew Punch

Seedless green grapes are best in this recipe because their more delicate flavor doesn't overwhelm the other ingredients.

INGREDIENTS | YIELDS 2 CUPS

½ cucumber
¼ small honeydew melon
1 cup seedless green grapes
2 kiwi fruits, peeled
¾ cup spinach
Sprig of mint
1 lemon, peeled

Grapes and Phytochemicals

All grapes are high in phytochemicals, plant-derived compounds that are not classified as vitamins or minerals but remain active in the body working to help prevent strokes, cancer, and diabetes.

1. Process the cucumber and melon through an electronic juicer according to the manufacturer's directions.

2. Add the grapes and the kiwis.

3. Add the spinach and the mint, followed by the lemon.

4. Mix the juice thoroughly to combine ingredients and serve immediately.

PER SERVING: Calories: 333 | Fat: 1.5g | Protein: 6.3g | Sodium: 79mg | Carbohydrates: 84g | Sugar: 47g

Magic Medicine

Winnie-the-Pooh knew what's what. The raw honey used in this recipe has antibacterial qualities and can contain antimicrobial properties. It's been found useful for digestion, bronchitis, and increased energy and longevity. If you think of your body as an engine, raw, unrefined honey qualifies as one of the super fuels.

INGREDIENTS | YIELDS 1 CUP

1 mango, peeled and cored
½ cup peaches
½ cup pineapple chunks
2 tablespoons raw honey
1 teaspoon fresh grated ginger
1 cup blueberries

Mango Mania?

Everything about the mango has medicinal properties. The roots and bark are anti-inflammatory. The leaves have astringent and styptic properties. The flowers help to increase red blood cells. The fruits help with digestion and help to reduce gas. The seed kernel is effective against parasites and is thought to act as a tonic on the female organs.

1. Process the mango through your electronic juicer according to the manufacturer's directions.

2. Add the peaches and pineapples chunks, a few at a time.

3. Mix the honey with the ginger and blueberries and add to the juicer.

4. Mix the juice thoroughly before serving.

PER SERVING: Calories: 425 | Fat: 1.5g | Protein: 3.5g | Sodium: 9mg | Carbohydrates: 110g | Sugar: 94g

Night on the Town Tonic

Whether it's a holiday special, a family celebration, or an all-nighter with friends, even the best of us overindulge on occasion. So whether you spent the night partying, wake up with the world's worst hangover, or last night's seven-course meal is still weighing heavy in your belly, this is the one to restore your good humor, digestive health, and reboot your system's healthy balance.

INGREDIENTS | YIELDS 2½ CUPS (2 SERVINGS)

1 small beet
6 medium carrots, trimmed
1 green pepper, seeded
1 red bell pepper, seeded
½ cup kale
2 cups baby spinach leaves
3 large tomatoes
¼ head fresh cabbage
3 stalks celery
4 green onions, trimmed
1 small clove garlic, peeled
1 teaspoon salt
Hot pepper sauce, to taste

1. Process the beet and the carrots through your electronic juicer according to the manufacturer's directions.

2. Add the peppers, followed by the kale and spinach.

3. Add the tomatoes, cabbage, and celery

4. Last, add the onions and garlic and salt.

5. Whisk the juice thoroughly to combine, season to taste with hot sauce, and serve over ice to increase hydration.

PER SERVING: Calories: 468 | Fat: 3.8g | Protein: 18g | Sodium: 2,357mg | Carbohydrates: 103g | Sugar: 57g

Don't Procrastinate!

Always remember that the nutrients in fresh juice are fragile. Every minute the juice stands, you lose enzymes and other micronutrients. Retain the full benefits of your freshly made juice by drinking your power cocktails as soon as possible after you make them.

Up and At 'Em

Just not a morning person? If you're the type who has to drink a pot of coffee before you can make a pot of coffee, this uncomplicated juice is easy to make and will get you going faster than you ever thought possible!

INGREDIENTS | YIELDS 1½ CUPS

3 carrots, trimmed
1 apple, cored
2 medium oranges, peeled
1 (1-inch) piece fresh ginger

All about Ginger

Fresh ginger is great for the digestion, but did you also know it's great for circulation and improves blood flow to the brain? A piece held under the tongue is also helpful in curing motion sickness and the nausea that can accompany rough airline flights or boat trips.

1. Process the carrots and the apple through your electronic juicer according to the manufacturer's directions.

2. Add the oranges, a few sections at a time.

3. Add the ginger.

4. Mix the juice thoroughly and enjoy!

PER SERVING: Calories: 257 | Fat: 1g | Protein: 4g | Sodium: 149mg | Carbohydrates: 64g | Sugar: 44g

Stress Buster

If good health is the goal, stress is its enemy. This one helps to offset the effects of stress.

INGREDIENTS | YIELDS 1½ CUPS

½ honeydew melon, peeled
1 cup watermelon chunks
1 orange, peeled

How to Pick a Melon

You've probably heard about melon thumping as a measure of ripeness, but there are others, too. One of the best for cantaloupe and honeydew melons is simply to smell them. If they don't smell like melon, they're not ripe. Same holds true of peaches and nectarines.

1. Process the fruits in any order through an electronic juicing machine according to the manufacturer's directions.

2. Whisk the juice to combine ingredients and enjoy!

PER SERVING: Calories: 287 | Fat: 1g | Protein: 4.8g | Sodium: 91mg | Carbohydrates: 72g | Sugar: 62g

Ginger Zinger

Another great choice for your morning wakeup call.

INGREDIENTS | YIELDS 1 CUP

3 medium Granny Smith apples, cored
½ medium cucumber
1 (1-inch) piece of ginger

1. Process the apple through your electronic juicer according to the manufacturer's directions.

2. Add the cucumber and ginger.

3. Mix the juice thoroughly and enjoy!

PER SERVING: Calories: 312 | Fat: 1g | Protein: 2.5g | Sodium: 9mg | Carbohydrates: 82g | Sugar: 59g

Relaxing Cooler

Some phytonutrients in fruits and vegetables actually help muscles and blood vessels relax. This is a great one to try at the end of a hectic day or a long workout.

INGREDIENTS | YIELDS 2½ CUPS (2 SERVINGS)

4 apples, cored
2 cups sweet cherries, pitted
1 cup blueberries
½ lemon, peeled

1. Process the apples through an electronic juicer according to manufacturer's directions.

2. Add the cherries, followed by the blueberries and the lemon.

3. Whisk the juice to blend, and serve alone or over ice.

PER SERVING: Calories: 488 | Fat: 1.5g | Protein: 5.8g | Sodium: 2mg | Carbohydrates: 129g | Sugar: 99g

Lemon Zest

Lemon juice really helps perk up the flavor of sweet juices like this. By adding a note of tartness, the sweetness is enhanced.

CHAPTER 3

Juices for Detox and Cleansing

For a lot of people, detoxification and cleansing have become a regular ritual, rather like spring cleaning your house. But any discussion of detoxing needs to begin with a couple of questions: First, what exactly is detoxification, and second, why do you need it?

Fact is, your body is eliminating toxins all the time. It's the normal physical process of eliminating or neutralizing toxins through your organs including the colon, liver, kidneys, lungs, lymph glands, and even your skin. Metabolic processes continually dispose of toxic matter.

Helping the Body Remove Toxins

Why do you need to remove toxins if your body does it naturally? It's no secret that people are exposed to more environmental toxins than ever before. Chemicals in the air you breathe, pesticides in the foods you eat, pollutants in your water, and increased exposure to synthetic substances can be more than the average person can handle. When enough toxins aren't eliminated, it can set the stage for disease. Toxins the body can't manage to eliminate or doesn't know what to do with are often stored in your fat cells, which is one of the big reasons why excess weight is generally seen as unhealthy and why a fat-reducing program is also seen as playing a big part in detoxification.

Unhealthy living habits such as not getting enough exercise or sleep, stress, poor diet, and even some medications can all reduce the body's efficiency at eliminating toxins. Demanding schedules and busy lifestyles also mean you can't just check into the spa whenever you're feeling a little blah, either.

While a number of experts insist that there's no scientific evidence to support the notion that more stringent detox regimens, cleanses, and fasts yield miraculous results, even the most skeptical agree that there are things anyone can do to help speed up the body's elimination systems. And one of those is juicing regularly.

So again, while juicing isn't a magic wand that will restore good health, vitality, and eliminate all your bad habits, it can play a valuable role in keeping the body operating at maximum efficiency.

Six Signs You Need to Detox

Many doctors recommend that everyone needs to detox at least once a year. You can choose a short fast or simply take a few days to refuel and reboot with healthy foods and nutrients.

FACT

Many traditions around the world celebrate the New Year with healthier cuisine than the holiday season might provide. In the American South, a simple New Year's meal consists of collard greens and black-eyed peas. In Italy, lentils are on the menu. But it's no accident that such traditions have evolved. Legumes are rich in cleansing fiber, and collard greens are rich in vitamins, folates, sulforaphane, and antioxidants, all essential elements of a detox regimen.

No matter what time of year though, listen to your body and watch for the following clues that it may be the right time to do some detoxing.

- Lack of energy, sluggishness, confusion, or fatigue that has no obvious explanation
- Irritated skin, rashes, complexion upsets
- Eruptions of herpes, shingles, psoriasis, or eczema
- Menstrual difficulties
- Bowel irregularity
- Distended stomach, even if you're otherwise thin

Detox Juices

The Detox Special

Any worthwhile detox regimen will pay special attention to fruits and veggies that benefit the liver. Not only is it the largest organ in the body, it's one of the most important for its abilities to eliminate toxins, filter the blood, metabolize nutrients, and hundreds of other functions.

INGREDIENTS | YIELDS 1 CUP

3 medium sugar beets, including greens, trimmed

1 medium carrot, trimmed

½ pound black seedless grapes

1. Cut the beets and greens into pieces.

2. Process the beets, greens, and carrot through your electronic juicer according to the manufacturer's directions.

3. Add the grapes.

4. Whisk the juice to combine the ingredients completely. Drink immediately.

PER SERVING: Calories: 289 | Fat: 1g | Protein: 6g | Sodium: 246mg | Carbohydrates: 70g | Sugar: 54g

Borscht in a Glass

Add plain yogurt to this recipe for a more authentic borscht experience!

INGREDIENTS | YIELDS 1 CUP

2 small sugar beets, including greens

1 medium apple, cored

1 medium orange, peeled and segmented

3 green onions, including tops

1 large cucumber

2 tablespoons fresh mint leaves

Beet Greens

Like beets themselves, beet greens are a powerful cleanser of the liver, blood, and kidneys. Beet juice and juice made with beet greens should always be taken in moderation and always combined with other ingredients to avoid the ill effects sometimes associated with a high oxalic acid content.

1. Process the beets and greens through your electronic juicer according to the manufacturer's directions.

2. Add the apple, followed by the orange segments.

3. Add the onions and cucumber.

4. Add the mint leaves.

5. Mix the juice thoroughly to combine and serve over ice.

PER SERVING: Calories: 220 | Fat: 1g | Protein: 5g | Sodium: 138mg | Carbohydrates: 53g | Sugar: 39g

Glamorous Greens

Watercress and arugula both help activate enzymes in the liver, while acting as a natural diuretic. Plus, they contribute a lively, peppery flavor that makes this one taste like it's fresh from the spa!

INGREDIENTS | YIELDS 1½ CUPS

½ bunch spinach, about 2 cups

1 cup watercress

1 cup arugula

1 medium apple, cored

½ lemon, peeled

2 stalks celery, with leaves

½ inch slice of fresh ginger

Juicing Greens

To make juicing green leafy vegetables like lettuce and spinach easier, roll the greens into balls before adding to the juicer.

1. Rinse the spinach, watercress, and arugula well to ensure greens are free of grit.

2. Process the apple through an electronic juicer according to the manufacturer's directions.

3. Add the lemon and celery stalks.

4. Add the greens and ginger in any order.

5. Whisk the juice to combine and serve well-chilled or over ice.

PER SERVING: Calories: 148 | Fat: 1g | Protein: 7.5g | Sodium: 218mg | Carbohydrates: 33g | Sugar: 19g

Pomegranate Power

Some scholars believe Eve actually ate a pomegranate she plucked from the tree of knowledge in the Garden of Eden, not an apple. Ancient Egyptians buried the dead with pomegranates because they believe those who ate the fruit would be blessed with eternal life.

INGREDIENTS | YIELDS 1 CUP

4 pomegranates, peeled
½ lemon, peeled
2 tablespoons raw honey

Pomegranate Powers

Pomegranates are full of antioxidants, believed to prevent blood clots, and can lower levels of bad cholesterol. They're also good for the heart, and help fight prostate cancer and erectile dysfunction. When juicing, it's best to peel the fruits, taking care to remove the white portions, which can be bitter. Be sure to include the seeds though, where some powerful nutrients are stored. If they seem tough to peel, score the rind and soak for 10 minutes in plain water.

1. Process the peeled pomegranates through an electronic juicer according to the manufacturer's directions.

2. Add the lemon.

3. Add the honey to the resulting juice.

4. Whisk the juice until the honey is completely dissolved and enjoy!

PER SERVING: Calories: 426 | Fat: 4g | Protein: 6g | Sodium: 12mg | Carbohydrates: 101g | Sugar: 83g

Boosting Body Cleanse

One of the first places the need for detox shows up is in the complexion. This one is especially recommended for calming down skin flare ups and restoring a healthy glow.

INGREDIENTS | YIELDS 1 CUP

1 cup broccoli florets

3 medium carrots, trimmed

1 medium apple, such as Granny Smith, cored

1 celery stalk, including leaves

½ cup spinach leaves

Cheers to Broccoli!

Less than 50 calories worth of broccoli contains more than 150 percent of our daily requirements of vitamin C, 60 percent of vitamin A, 5 percent of iron, and 5 percent of calcium. It's also rich in sulforaphane, an enzyme that is essential in removing potentially harmful carcinogens from the body. Finally, other phytonutrients help protect and balance estrogen cells, which some scientists believe are particularly susceptible to cancer-causing agents.

1. Process the broccoli, carrots, and apple through an electronic juicer according to the manufacturer's directions.

2. Add the celery stalk and spinach leaves.

3. Mix the juice thoroughly and drink as soon as possible after preparation for maximum effect.

PER SERVING: Calories: 206 | Fat: 1g | Protein: 5g | Sodium: 222mg | Carbohydrates: 49g | Sugar: 28g

Iron Man (or Woman)

Truth is, many more women tend to suffer from low iron and anemia than men do. Symptoms of a low red blood cell count can include fatigue, decreased energy, and dizziness. One of the principal causes of low iron is poor nutrition, so be sure to include this iron booster in your body's good housekeeping plan.

INGREDIENTS | YIELDS 3 CUPS (2 SERVINGS)

4 large oranges, peeled

4 medium lemons, peeled

¼ cup raw honey, or to taste

4 cups red, black, or green seedless grapes

Oranges for Juicing?

Some oranges are bred for ease of eating, like the easy peeling navel. But other oranges yield more juice. Valencia is a great choice, with Hamlins and blood oranges also favored to yield more juice per fruit.

1. Process the oranges and lemons in an electronic juicer according to the manufacturer's directions.

2. Add the honey, followed by the grapes.

3. Whisk the juice to combine completely and enjoy! If you prefer, add cold water to thin the juice slightly and lessen the intensity of the flavor.

PER SERVING: Calories: 922 | Fat: 2g | Protein: 10g | Sodium: 20mg | Carbohydrates: 245g | Sugar: 204g

Total Body Detox

Veggies such as asparagus and celery are natural diuretics that are especially beneficial to the kidneys, another of the body's most important organs. This one is especially useful for those suffering side effects from certain medications.

INGREDIENTS | YIELDS 1 CUP

1 large tomato
2 stalks asparagus
1 medium cucumber
½ lemon, peeled

Asparagus: A Super Food

Thought to be one of the superfoods, asparagus will not, as some sources insist, cure cancer. But it is extremely rich in folic acid, vitamins A and E, and iron.

1. Process the tomato and asparagus through your electronic juicer according to the manufacturer's directions.

2. Add the cucumber and lemon.

3. Mix the juice to combine and served chilled or over ice.

PER SERVING: Calories: 91 | Fat: 1g | Protein: 4.5g | Sodium: 16mg | Carbohydrates: 21g | Sugar: 10g

Carrot Cleanse

It seems as though everyone has a favorite juice when it comes to cleansing and detoxifying, but you can't go wrong with carrots. They are especially beneficial for colon health, and are a rich source of vitamin A, which is essential to the health of all the mucous membranes of the body. The addition of lemon to this recipe adds vitamin C and balances the carrots with a brighter note of flavor.

INGREDIENTS | YIELDS 1 CUP

½ pound carrots, trimmed

1 large apple, cored

1 lemon, peeled and seeded

Toxic Toppers

Unlike other root veggies such as beets and turnips, never use carrot greens in your juice. They are not only bitter, they contain elements that can be toxic.

1. Process the carrots, one at a time, through your electronic juicer according to the manufacturer's directions.

2. Cut the apple into chunks and add.

3. Add the lemon.

4. Whisk the juice to combine and enjoy immediately.

PER SERVING: Calories: 212 | Fat: 1g | Protein: 3.5g | Sodium: 155mg | Carbohydrates: 54g | Sugar: 33g

Artichoke Cilantro Cocktail

This juice uses Jerusalem artichokes, a root vegetable related to the sunflower family. Sometimes called sun chokes or earth apples, they can be found in organic and specialty markets.
This is an intensely flavored juice, so add distilled water as desired.

INGREDIENTS | YIELDS 1 CUP

4 Jerusalem artichokes
1 bunch fresh cilantro, about 1 cup
4 large radishes, tailed and trimmed
3 medium carrots, trimmed

Cilantrophobia

Cilantro is the fresh leaves of the coriander plant. Sometimes known as Chinese parsley, its strong aroma and unusual flavor tends to polarize opinion on its use as a seasoning. Food scientists believe that whether you like it or hate it may have something to do with genetics. Famous chef Julia Child was once quoted as saying she would just pick it out and throw it on the floor!

1. Process the Jerusalem artichokes, one at a time, through your electronic juicer according to the manufacturer's directions.

2. Roll the cilantro into a ball to compress and add.

3. Add the radishes and carrots.

4. Mix the juice thoroughly to combine and serve over ice as desired.

PER SERVING: Calories: 303 | Fat: 0.5g | Protein: 8g | Sodium: 159mg | Carbohydrates: 71g | Sugar: 38g

C-Water Detox

Don't forget that good old aqua pura is one of the best and most efficient ways to detox and cleanse your body. The recipe uses kiwi and grapefruit for a nice vitamin C blast as well.

INGREDIENTS | YIELDS 1½ CUPS

3 kiwi fruit
2 pink grapefruits, peeled and seeded
4 ounces water

Peel It?

Despite the kiwi's fuzzy exterior, it really isn't necessary to peel them before processing. If you find the fuzz too off-putting, scrub the fruit lightly with a brush to remove it before juicing.

1. Process the kiwi and the grapefruit through your electronic juicer according to the manufacturer's directions.

2. Add the water and mix thoroughly.

3. Drink as soon as possible after preparation as fresh vitamin C deteriorates quickly.

PER SERVING: Calories: 302 | Fat: 1.5g | Protein: 5.5g | Sodium: 14mg | Carbohydrates: 75g | Sugar: 35g

Papaya Strawberry Cleanse

Papaya is a great cleansing fruit and is good for people with liver problems, constipation, and urinary disorders.

INGREDIENTS | YIELDS 1¼ CUPS

2 papayas
1 cup strawberries, hull intact

What Is Papain?

Papayas contain papain, a digestive enzyme that is used in meat tenderizers to break down tough meat fibers. South Americans have used papain to tenderize meat for centuries, and it is now available in powdered meat tenderizers all over the world. Papaya is a very good source of vitamins A and C.

1. Process the papayas and strawberries through your electronic juicer according to the manufacturer's directions.

2. Stir together and enjoy!

PER SERVING: Calories: 283 | Fat: 1.2g | Protein: 4.6g | Sodium: 19mg | Carbohydrates: 70g | Sugar: 42g

Apple Cucumber Cocktail

When it comes to body cleansing, sometimes the simplest combinations are the best. Cucumbers are not only a good diuretic, which helps flush the kidneys, they also help to control arthritis, eczema, and remove toxins from the blood.

INGREDIENTS | YIELDS 1 CUP

1 medium cucumber
1 medium apple, cored
Water to make 1 cup juice

How Much to Buy?

In juicing, a good rule of thumb to follow when calculating how much produce you need to buy is: 1 pound produce will yield approximately 1 cup of juice.

1. Process the cucumber and the apple through your electronic juicer according to the manufacturer's directions.

2. Add the water to make 1 cup and mix thoroughly. Drink and enjoy!

PER SERVING: Calories: 122 | Fat: 0.5g | Protein: 2.4g | Sodium: 6mg | Carbohydrates: 31g | Sugar: 21g

Avocado Smoothie

Avocados don't juice well, but can be blended with fresh pressed juice for an elegant smoothie. In hospitals, avocados are often blended with infant formula or breast milk and fed to premature infants with immature digestive systems to help build them up.

INGREDIENTS | YIELDS 1½ CUPS

2 leaves kale or Swiss chard, chopped
½ cup mango chunks
¼ avocado
½ cup coconut water
½ cup ice

The Awesome Avocado

Avocados contain more than 20 nutrients, are rich in vitamin K and monosaturated fats, and are thought to assist in reducing high blood pressure and bad cholesterol.

1. Process the kale or Swiss chard and the mango chunks through an electronic juicer according to the manufacturer's directions.

2. Transfer the mixture to a blender and add the avocado, coconut water, and ice.

3. Blend until smooth.

PER SERVING: Calories: 201 | Fat: 8.5g | Protein: 6g | Sodium: 62mg | Fiber: 7.5g | Carbohydrates: 31g | Sugar: 12g

Minty Melon Cleanser

All melons are good for a cleanse because of their high water content. Cantaloupe is especially good with its high carotene content.

INGREDIENTS | YIELDS 1½ CUPS

½ cantaloupe, peeled and seeded
¼ cup fresh mint leaves
¼ cup parsley
1 cup blueberries

Always Use Alkaline

Juice from alkaline vegetables including carrots, tomatoes, parsley, spinach, kale, and celery helps detoxify the liver, kidneys, blood, and muscle tissue of toxins that have been accumulating for years.

1. Cut the melon into chunks and process through an electronic juicer according to the manufacturer's directions.

2. Roll the mint and parsley into balls to compress and add to the juicer.

3. Add the blueberries.

4. Whisk the juice together to combine ingredients and enjoy!

PER SERVING: Calories: 193 | Fat: 1.2g | Protein: 4.6g | Sodium: 60mg | Carbohydrates: 46g | Sugar: 36g

Cranapple Magic

Why buy bottled when you can make this yourself?

INGREDIENTS | YIELDS 1½ CUPS

¾ cup cranberries
3 medium carrots, trimmed
2 apples, cored

Craving Cranberries?

Scientists have discovered that cranberries contain an amazing array of phytonutrients that include flavonoids, phenolic acids, and anthocyanins, all powerful antioxidants that help prevent cancer, infections, and may help to prevent ailments such as stomach ulcers.

1. Process the cranberries through an electronic juicer according to the manufacturer's directions.

2. Add the carrots and the apples.

3. Mix the juice thoroughly and serve.

PER SERVING: Calories: 277 | Fat: 1g | Protein: 3g | Sodium: 150mg | Carbohydrates: 70g | Sugar: 45g

Three, Two, One!

Countdown your cleanse with this easy recipe. The high fiber content of this combo will help readjust your digestion to solid foods as you're coming off a fast.

INGREDIENTS | YIELDS 1½ CUPS

3 apples, cored
2 carrots, trimmed
1 yam, peeled

Yams, a Rich Source of Vitamin K

Most people are aware that vitamin K is essential to proper blood clotting, but you may not know that it also contributes to heart and bone health.

1. Process the apples through an electronic juicer according to the manufacturer's directions.

2. Add the carrots, followed by the yam.

3. Whisk the juice to combine the ingredients and serve alone or over ice.

PER SERVING: Calories: 408 | Fat: 1g | Protein: 4.2g | Sodium: 82mg | Carbohydrates: 101g | Sugar: 45g

Cabbage Kale Cleanse

Not just for cleansing, cabbage has beneficial effects for hair, skin, and nails, too!

INGREDIENTS | YIELDS 1½ CUPS

1 cup broccoli florets
1 small head red cabbage
3 large leaves kale or Swiss chard

Swiss Chard

There are several varieties of chards available, and while they carry many of the nutritional benefits of kale, many juicers prefer it because it has a milder flavor.

1. Process the broccoli through an electronic juicer according to the manufacturer's directions.

2. Cut the cabbage into chunks and add to the juicer.

3. Add the kale or chard.

4. Mix the juice thoroughly and serve alone or over ice.

PER SERVING: Calories: 242 | Fat: 1.5g | Protein: 14g | Sodium: 187mg | Carbohydrates: 54g | Sugar: 24g

Yamtastic

If juice fasting leaves you a bit low on get up and go, use this juice for an energy boost!

INGREDIENTS | YIELDS 1½ CUPS

3 oranges, peeled
2 Anjou pears, cored
1 large yam, peeled

Not the Same

Although similar in taste, yams and sweet potatoes don't belong to the same botanical family. Yams are closely related to the lily, while sweet potatoes belong to the Morning Glory family.

1. Process the orange segments through an electronic juicer according to the manufacturer's directions.

2. Add the pears.

3. Cut the yam into pieces and add to the juicer. Serve over ice.

PER SERVING: Calories: 484 | Fat: 1g | Protein: 6g | Sodium: 16mg | Carbohydrates: 121g | Sugar: 56g

The Crucible

Named for this concoction of cruciferous vegetables. All members of the cabbage family, they're rich in the vitamins, mineral, and fiber believed essential to preventing and fighting cancer.

INGREDIENTS | YIELDS 1½ CUPS

1 stalk broccoli
¼ head cabbage
¼ head cauliflower
2 kale leaves
½ lemon, peeled
2 apples, cored

Broccoli Caution

If you're a type 2 diabetic, consult with your doctor about juicing. Broccoli juice has been seen to interfere with some diabetic medications.

1. Process the broccoli segments through an electronic juicer according to the manufacturer's directions.

2. Add the cabbage, followed by the cauliflower.

3. Add the kale, followed by the lemon and the apples.

4. Whisk the juice together to combine and serve over ice.

PER SERVING: Calories: 291 | Fat: 2g | Protein: 13g | Sodium: 163mg | Carbohydrates: 67g | Sugar: 35g

Cinnamon Cider

The addition of cinnamon in this recipe is useful for controlling blood pressure.

INGREDIENTS | YIELDS 1½ CUPS

2 apples, cored
8 stalks celery
Dash of cinnamon

1. Process the apples through an electronic juicer according to the manufacturer's directions.

2. Add the celery. Add the cinnamon to the resulting juice.

3. Whisk the juice together to combine and serve immediately.

PER SERVING: Calories: 132 | Fat: 0.5g | Protein: 1.6g | Sodium: 109mg | Carbohydrates: 33g | Sugar: 24g

Root Vegetable Cleanse

Root vegetables are a staple on any juice fast because of their soluble fiber.

INGREDIENTS | YIELDS 1½ CUPS

½ medium beet, tailed and trimmed
3 medium carrots, trimmed
2 apples, cored
1 medium sweet potato, cut into chunks
¼ sweet Spanish or Vidalia onion, peeled

1. Process the beet and carrots through an electronic juicer according to the manufacturer's directions.

2. Add the apples and sweet potato, followed by the onion.

3. Mix the juice thoroughly to combine ingredients and serve immediately.

PER SERVING: Calories: 307 | Fat: 0.8g | Protein: 5g | Sodium: 208mg | Carbohydrates: 75g | Sugar: 38g

Mango Tea

The fresh juice of mango mixed with an herbal tea of your choice provides a really great tasting tea that's good for detoxing.

INGREDIENTS | YIELDS 2 CUPS

½ mango, peeled and seeded
1 cup hot water
1 herbal tea bag

1. Process the mango through an electronic juicer according to the manufacturer's directions.

2. Pour water over the tea bag and let steep for 2 minutes.

3. Add ¼ cup mango juice to the tea and stir.

PER SERVING: Calories: 69 | Fat: 0.2g | Protein: 0.6g | Sodium: 18mg | Carbohydrates: 18g | Sugar: 15g

Herbal Teas

Herbal teas have been around for many years and have been used to treat a variety of health problems. They are also known for their earthy taste and soothing effect. There is a wide variety of herbal teas available in the market, some especially recommended for the detoxification process. As well as being delicious and nutritious, herbal teas are often caffeine-free.

CHAPTER 4

Juicing for Weight Loss

There's been an awful lot of hype on the subject of juicing and its relationship to weight loss. Juice and juicing has become all the rage in celebrity circles and it seems like there's a new juice diet every week. But just as you wouldn't buy a car from somebody who doesn't know how to drive, taking diet advice from svelte celebs who've never had a real weight problem is probably not such a great idea. First and foremost, juicing is only one aspect of a comprehensive weight loss program. You still have to exercise, you still have to eat the right kinds of foods, and above all, avoid the temptation to "binge" on the fattening stuff one day, then "purge" with a juice fast the next. That's the sort of habit that can wreak havoc with your digestion and your metabolism, as well as decrease your chances of lasting results. It's always a good idea to consult with your health practitioner to rule out any pre-existing conditions or health problems.

You *Will* Lose Weight by Juicing Regularly

The good news is, it's true, even by juicing only three or four times a week, you can expect to eliminate pounds of excess water weight and waste that may have been stored in the bowels. Further, your increased energy levels may help to metabolize your food faster. But to take weight loss to the next level, you need to burn fat.

How do you do that? If you want to lose weight, you have to take in fewer calories than your body needs. The amount of calories your body needs depends on factors such as your age, sex, level of activity, and so forth. So let's say you need 2,000 calories a day. When you only consume 1,200 or 1,500—then your body isn't getting enough fuel to have the energy to maintain your normal, active life. Your system will then have to get the energy it needs from your stored fat cells. So if you eat 500 calories less than your normal requirement each day, it's enough to help you lose a pound per week. And that can add up to a significant weight loss over time.

Where does juicing fit in? Juice is extremely low in calories, provides a host of essential nutrients, and can contain enough soluble fiber and simple sugars to help you "feel full." It's an effective and easy-to-prepare meal or snack substitute that's low in calories, delicious, and a very healthy way to eliminate those 500 calories without even missing them!

Which Fruits and Vegetables Are Best for Weight Loss?

Let's face it: No weight loss program is going to be very effective if you just don't like what you're supposed to be consuming. So when choosing fruits and vegetables for weight loss juicing, the first thing to consider is that it's important to choose what you like. If the mere idea of kale makes you turn up your nose, or kiwis give you the heebie-jeebies, then it doesn't make sense to include those things in your weight loss repertoire of juice ingredients.

At the same time, variety is everything. Many a well-meaning dieter has given into temptation, just because they weren't giving their senses enough flavor, color, and delicious smelling stimulation. Be sure to include fruits to ward off sugar cravings and veggies with enough fiber, such as carrots or cabbage, to keep you feeling full. Fortunately, nature has provided us with infinite possible combinations of produce, so feel free to experiment and explore those concoctions that are especially appealing to the nose, the eye, and the palate.

Keep in mind though that when it comes to weight loss, all fruits and vegetables are not necessarily created equal. Some have more nutrients per calorie than others, to give your body what it needs. When the body gets enough of what it needs, you're automatically going to feel better physically, and emotionally as well.

At the risk of sounding repetitious, the absolute best vegetables to help speed up weight loss are the green vegetables: chard, kale, bok choy, collard greens, spinach, cabbage, Brussels sprouts, and broccoli. Others that will help with both their nutrient values and diuretic properties are the lettuces, tomatoes, celery, and bell peppers.

By the same token, some fruits are considered better for weight loss than others. These include many of the superfoods, like oranges and apples. But for fruits, the real stars of the weight loss team are the berries. Strawberries, raspberries, and blueberries top the list, followed by acai and goji berries. When choosing fruits for weight loss, always look for those with a high vitamin C content, such as kiwi or grapefruit. Vitamin C helps to flush the system of the waste that is produced as fat cells burn.

Essential Juices
for Weight Loss

Citrus Blueberry Blend

If you prefer a less tart juice and want more of the blueberry flavor to come through, use another orange and only half the grapefruit. If you prefer a more tart juice, use white grapefruit.

INGREDIENTS | YIELDS 1 CUP

1 cup blueberries
2 oranges, peeled
1 pink grapefruit, peeled

1. Process the fruits through the feed tube of an electronic juicer according to the manufacturer's directions in any order you wish.

2. Drink as soon as possible after preparation.

PER SERVING: Calories: 238 | Fat: 1g | Protein: 4g | Sodium: 1.5mg | Carbohydrates: 60g | Sugar: 46g

Grapefruit and Dieters

Adding grapefruit to your diet is believed to assist in weight loss through an enzyme that acts with protein to regulate insulin levels and control hunger pangs. One study funded by the Florida Department of Citrus found that the addition of a half grapefruit or 4 ounces of juice with meals resulted in an average weight loss of more than three pounds in twelve weeks, with some participants losing as much as ten pounds.

Watermelon Orange Juice

This delicious juice reduces cravings for sugary snacks and is great for dumping excess water weight.

INGREDIENTS | YIELDS 1½ CUPS

2 cups watermelon chunks
1 large orange, peeled

1. Process the fruits through an electronic juicer according to the manufacturer's directions.

2. Serve alone or over ice.

PER SERVING: Calories: 136 | Fat: 0.6g | Protein: 2.7g | Sodium: 3mg | Carbohydrates: 34g | Sugar: 27g

Berry Beet Special

Substitute milk or yogurt for the water in this recipe for a smoothie variation.

INGREDIENTS | YIELDS 1 CUP

1 cup blueberries
½ cup strawberries
½ medium beet
1 large leaf rainbow chard
½ cup spring water

1. Process the berries through an electronic juicer according to the manufacturer's directions.

2. Add the beet and the chard.

3. Whisk the juice together with the water to blend and enjoy!

PER SERVING: Calories: 131 | Fat: 0.8g | Protein: 2.8g | Sodium: 110mg | Carbohydrates: 32g | Sugar: 21g

Sassy Snack

Celery is a great diuretic, spinach is full of iron, and the sweet potato in this recipe is sure to fill you up when your stomach is telling you it's time to eat!

INGREDIENTS | YIELDS 1½ CUPS

1 sweet potato, peeled
4 stalks celery, with leaves
½ cup spinach
1 zucchini
1 cucumber

1. Cut the sweet potato into chunks and process through an electronic juicer according to the manufacturer's directions.

2. Add the celery and spinach.

3. Cut the zucchini into chunks and add it to the juicer, followed by the cucumber.

4. Whisk the juice thoroughly to combine and serve over ice as desired.

PER SERVING: Calories: 219 | Fat: 1.4g | Protein: 8g | Sodium: 233mg | Carbohydrates: 48g | Sugar: 18g

Weight Goal Shake

Definitely a substitute for lunch or dinner, 2 or 3 glasses of this per week and you'll reach your weight goal in no time! Two servings make this ideal for sharing with a weight loss juice buddy, too!

INGREDIENTS | YIELDS 2½ CUPS
(2 SERVINGS)

1 medium sugar beet, tops optional
5 carrots, trimmed
2 stalks celery, including leaves
1 cucumber, cut into chunks
1 grapefruit, peeled
1 kiwi
1 plum, pitted
2 pears, cored
2 apples, cored

Alternating Ingredients

When using a recipe like this one, which includes quite a few ingredients, always alternate harder fruits and veggies with softer ones to avoid overworking your juicer.

1. Process the beet and carrots through an electronic juicer according to the manufacturer's directions.

2. Add the celery and cucumber.

3. Add the grapefruit and kiwi, followed by the plum.

4. Add the pears and apples.

5. Whisk or shake the juice to combine the ingredients. Serve straight up or over ice.

PER SERVING: Calories: 606 | Fat: 2.4g | Protein: 10g | Sodium: 276mg | Carbohydrates: 152g | Sugar: 94g

Apple Watermelon Punch

Great for losing excess water weight, this juice also gives you that "full" feeling.

INGREDIENTS | YIELDS 1½ CUPS

2 apples, cored
3 cups watermelon, cut into chunks

1. Process the apples through an electronic juicer according to the manufacturer's directions.

2. Add the watermelon.

3. Whisk the juice together to combine and serve immediately.

PER SERVING: Calories: 242 | Fat: 1g | Protein: 3.4g | Sodium: 4.5mg | Carbohydrates: 62g | Sugar: 50g

Juice for Supper Cocktail

When juicing for weight loss, sweeter juices in the evening help fight fatigue and keep up energy levels until bedtime rolls around.

INGREDIENTS | YIELDS 1½ CUPS

1 medium apple, cored
¼ honeydew melon, peeled and seeded
½ cup raspberries
1 medium pear, cored

Great Flavor Combos
The predominant notes of pear and raspberry in the recipe complement each other perfectly and are nicely rounded out by the apple and melon. For a special treat, serve in an elegantly iced martini or margarita glass that's been prechilled in the freezer.

1. Process the apple through an electronic juicer according to the manufacturer's directions.

2. Add the melon, cut into chunks, followed by the raspberries.

3. Add the pear.

4. Whisk the juice to combine ingredients; serve in a chilled glass or over ice.

PER SERVING: Calories: 260 | Fat: 1g | Protein: 3g | Sodium: 47mg | Carbohydrates: 67g | Sugar: 48g

Sweet Shake

All the flavor of a fattening dessert, with none of the consequences!

INGREDIENTS | YIELDS 1 CUP

1 banana, frozen or fresh

1 apple, cored

½ cup coconut milk

¼ teaspoon nutmeg

1 teaspoon pumpkin pie spice

Bananas in the Blender

Use a bullet-type juicer or blender to combine pulpy fruits such as bananas and avocados.

1. Combine all the ingredients in a blender and purée until smooth.

2. Serve immediately.

PER SERVING: Calories: 373 | Fat: 24g | Protein: 3.8g | Sodium: 16mg | Carbohydrates: 42g | Sugar: 23g

Super Weight Loss Cocktail

Vary the greens in this recipe according to your tastes and the season.
It's guaranteed to fill you up, without filling you out!

INGREDIENTS | YIELDS 2 CUPS
(2 SERVINGS)

2 stalks celery, including leaves

½ cucumber

¼ head green cabbage

2 stalks bok choy

½ medium apple, cored

½ lemon, peeled

1 (½-inch) piece ginger

½ cup parsley

5 kale or collard leaves

1 cup spinach

1. Process the celery and cucumber through an electronic juicer according to the manufacturer's directions.

2. Cut the cabbage into chunks and add to the juicer, followed by the bok choy, apple, and lemon.

3. Add the ginger and parsley.

4. Add the kale or collards, and the spinach.

5. Serve alone or over ice.

PER SERVING: Calories: 214 | Fat: 2g | Protein: 11g | Sodium: 188mg | Carbohydrates: 47g | Sugar: 17g

Feel the Burn Fat Burner

*This hot and spicy concoction will perk up your taste buds and your metabolism.
Hot peppers help to speed up metabolic systems and increase circulation.*

**INGREDIENTS | YIELDS 2½ CUPS
(2 SERVINGS)**

2 large tomatoes, quartered

2 stalks celery

3 or 4 radishes, tailed and trimmed

1 sweet red bell pepper, seeded

1 yellow banana pepper, or 1 fresh
jalapeño pepper, seeded

3 green onions

½ teaspoon cayenne pepper

Generous dash of Tabasco sauce, or to
taste

1. Process the tomatoes and the celery through an electronic juicer according to the manufacturer's directions.

2. Add the radishes and peppers.

3. Add the green onions.

4. Add the cayenne and hot sauce.

5. Whisk the juice to combine and enjoy!

PER SERVING: Calories: 129 | Fat: 1.7g | Protein: 5.5g |
Sodium: 460mg | Carbohydrates: 26g | Sugar: 17g

Spice It Up!

Capsaicin is a chemical found in jalapeño, cayenne, and other varieties of hot peppers. It's thought to aid weight loss because eating or juicing the peppers temporarily stimulates your body to release more stress hormones, which speeds up the metabolism in response.

Cellulite Buster

Any juice with high diuretic properties is going to help eliminate cellulite by reducing the water content of fat cells, thereby lessening those dreaded "dimples."

INGREDIENTS | YIELDS 1 CUP

1 apple, cored
1 grapefruit, peeled
2 stalks celery, with leaves
½ cucumber
2 tablespoons fresh mint leaves

1. Process the apple through an electronic juicer according to the manufacturer's directions.

2. Add the grapefruit sections, followed by the celery.

3. Add the cucumber and mint leaves.

4. Whisk or shake the juice to blend and enjoy!

PER SERVING: Calories: 161 | Fat: 0.8g | Protein: 3.7g | Sodium: 78mg | Carbohydrates: 39g | Sugar: 29g

Weight Loss and Calcium

Many studies have proven there's a direct relationship between calcium intake and the ability to lose weight easily. It's one of the reasons it's more difficult to shed pounds as we age and calcium levels are depleted. So when juicing for weight loss, look for fruits and veggies with a high calcium content including spinach, broccoli, bok choy, oranges, and grapefruit.

Grapefruit Watercress Delight

Watercress was discovered in a recent study to be of special benefit to smokers in reducing DNA damage to white blood cells.

INGREDIENTS | YIELDS 1½ CUPS

2 grapefruits, peeled
½ cup watercress
3 or 4 sprigs of parsley

1. Process the grapefruits through an electronic juicer according to the manufacturer's directions.

2. Add the watercress and parsley.

3. Serve the juice alone or over ice.

PER SERVING: Calories: 130 | Fat: 0.5g | Protein: 3g | Sodium: 8.5mg | Carbohydrates: 32g | Sugar: 27g

Tropic Weight Loss Ade

Mango is highly rated as a weight loss aid, partially due to its high concentration of soluble fiber.

INGREDIENTS | YIELDS 1½ CUPS

2 mangoes, seeded
1 apple, cored
1 grapefruit, peeled
1 (½-inch) piece of ginger

Ginger Tips

Store ginger in your vegetable bin in the fridge to prolong freshness. It's also extremely useful in preventing the nausea associated with morning sickness during pregnancy.

1. Process the mangoes through an electronic juicer according to the manufacturer's directions.

2. Add the apple, followed by the grapefruit segments and the ginger.

3. Whisk or shake the juice to combine ingredients and serve.

PER SERVING: Calories: 447 | Fat: 2g | Protein: 4.6g | Sodium: 10mg | Carbohydrates: 115g | Sugar: 95g

Raspberry Apple Snack

Though red raspberries are the most common variety, raspberries can be either red, purple, gold, or black, with the golden variety ranking as the sweetest of all!

INGREDIENTS | YIELDS 1½ CUPS

2 cups raspberries
2 apples, cored
1 lime, peeled

1. Process the berries through an electronic juicer according to the manufacturer's directions.

2. Add the apples, followed by the lime.

3. Whisk or shake the juice to combine ingredients and serve alone or over ice.

PER SERVING: Calories: 302 | Fat: 2g | Protein: 4g | Sodium: 3.8mg | Carbohydrates: 77g | Sugar: 44g

Jicama Juice

Jicama, or yam bean, is an excellent source of oligofructose inulin, a soluble dietary fiber. Inulin is a zero calorie, sweet inert carbohydrate and does not metabolize in the human body, which makes this juice an ideal sweet snack for diabetics and dieters, because it helps you feel fuller, longer.

INGREDIENTS | YIELDS 1 CUP

1 whole jicama
2 cups spinach
½ medium beet
½ lemon, peeled
1 medium orange, peeled

1. Process the jicama through an electronic juicer according to the manufacturer's directions.

2. Add the spinach.

3. Add the beet, followed by the lemon and orange segments.

4. Whisk or shake the juice to combine ingredients and serve over ice, if desired.

PER SERVING: Calories: 223 | Fat: 0.8g | Protein: 6g | Sodium: 94mg | Carbohydrates: 52g | Sugar: 19g

Orange Bonanza

This juice will help lower your blood pressure, improve your mood, and sweep out toxins while shedding those pounds.

INGREDIENTS | YIELDS 2 CUPS

2 small sugar beets, trimmed and tailed
2 large oranges, peeled
½ lemon, peeled
1 large carrot, trimmed
2 cups spinach
2 celery stalks with leaves
1 (1-inch) piece fresh ginger

1. Process the beets through an electronic juicer according to the manufacturer's directions.

2. Add the orange segments, followed by the lemon.

3. Process the carrot, then add the spinach and celery. Add the ginger.

4. Whisk the juice to combine ingredients, serve immediately.

PER SERVING: Calories: 309 | Fat: 1.5g | Protein: 9g | Sodium: 289mg | Carbohydrates: 73g | Sugar: 51g

Minty Refresher

Fresh mint is not just good for your breath, it's great for your digestion.

INGREDIENTS | YIELDS 1 CUP

4 stalks celery, with leaves
1 apple, cored
5 sprigs of mint
1 lime, peeled

1. Process the celery through an electronic juicer according to the manufacturer's directions.

2. Add the apple, followed by the mint and lime.

3. Serve alone or over ice.

PER SERVING: Calories: 135 | Fat: 0.8g | Protein: 3g | Sodium: 137mg | Carbohydrates: 34g | Sugar: 20g

Luscious Limes

Between 1795 and 1815, some 1.6 million gallons of lime juice drastically reduced the mortality rate of seamen from scurvy. That's why British seamen became known as "limeys."

Liquid Cruciferous

Simply adding cruciferous veggies like broccoli, cauliflower, cabbage, and kale can give your weight loss juice recipes real fat-fighting clout.

INGREDIENTS | YIELDS 2 CUPS (2 SERVINGS)

2 small zucchini

¼ red cabbage

2 red apples, cored

4 kale leaves

½ cup cauliflower florets

1 cup blueberries

1 orange, peeled

½ medium cucumber

½ cup coconut water

Weight and Hormones

Hormone disruptors called xenoestrogens mimic the effect of natural estrogen, which affects fat storage in the body. Apart from adding to cancer risks, xenoestrogens are known to cause our bodies to store more fat than usual, while at the same time making it very difficult to lose extra weight. The phytochemicals contained in cruciferous veggies help metabolize and eliminate xenoestrogens, putting the body back in hormonal balance.

1. Process the zucchini through an electronic juicer according to the manufacturer's directions.

2. Add the cabbage, followed by the apples and kale.

3. Add cauliflower, followed by the blueberries and the orange.

4. Add the cucumber. Add the coconut water to the resulting juice.

5. Whisk the juice to combine and enjoy!

PER SERVING: Calories: 566 | Fat: 4g | Protein: 19g | Sodium: 194mg | Carbohydrates: 133g | Sugar: 76g

A Hidden Clove

The sweetness of the carrots will offset the strong taste of garlic, and the dill adds a touch of green. This juice is great for reducing water retention.

INGREDIENTS | YIELDS 1 CUP

4 carrots, peeled
2 garlic cloves, peeled
1 sprig baby dill

1. Process carrots and garlic through an electronic juicer according to the manufacturer's directions.

2. Garnish juice with baby dill.

PER SERVING: Calories: 91 | Fat: 0.5g | Protein: 2g | Sodium: 139mg | Carbohydrates: 21g | Sugar: 9g

Strawberry Tomato Temptation

This one may seem like a surprising combination of flavors, but it's terrific!

INGREDIENTS | YIELDS 1 CUP

1 cup strawberries
3 medium tomatoes
¼ cup fresh basil leaves

Lycopene

Tomatoes are among the richest natural sources of lycopene, a powerful antioxidant that is not only useful in fighting cancer but is believed to help prevent hardening of the arteries.

1. Process the berries through an electronic juicer according to the manufacturer's directions.

2. Add the tomatoes, followed by the basil leaves.

3. Serve in a chilled glass, or over ice as desired.

PER SERVING: Calories: 97 | Fat: 1g | Protein: 3.5g | Sodium: 15mg | Carbohydrates: 22g | Sugar: 14g

Slim Fest

*This one has so many of the right ingredients for losing weight,
you are all but guaranteed results!*

**INGREDIENTS | YIELDS 2½ CUPS
(2 SERVINGS)**

1 small to medium beet, trimmed and tailed
1 medium tomato
4 medium carrots, trimmed
4 Brussels sprouts
½ cup cauliflower florets
¾ cup broccoli florets
2 pears, cored
2 apples, cored
½ cup pineapple chunks

1. Process the first three ingredients through an electronic juicer according to the manufacturer's directions.

2. Add the Brussels sprouts, cauliflower, and broccoli.

3. Add the pears, followed by the apples and pineapple.

4. Whisk the juice to combine ingredients and serve alone or over ice!

PER SERVING: Calories: 632 | Fat: 2.5g | Protein: 13g | Sodium: 329mg | Carbohydrates: 157g | Sugar: 99g

Sugar Beet Surprise

*Filling and flavorful. The surprise is that the addition of mint
enhances the sweetness and flavor of this recipe.*

INGREDIENTS | YIELDS 1 CUP

2 small sugar beets, trimmed with greens
1 large Granny Smith apple, cored
¼ cup fresh mint

1. Process the beets and the apple through an electronic juicer according to the manufacturer's directions.

2. Add the mint.

3. Stir or shake the juice together with some ice and enjoy!

PER SERVING: Calories: 158 | Fat: 0.6g | Protein: 4g | Sodium: 136mg | Carbohydrates: 38g | Sugar: 26g

Basil Blast

Better than a trip to the Mediterranean! Well, maybe not quite . . .

INGREDIENTS | YIELDS 1½ CUPS

1 cup fresh basil leaves
4 Roma tomatoes
1 clove garlic, peeled
½ medium cucumber

1. Process the basil and tomatoes through an electronic juicer according to the manufacturer's directions.

2. Add the garlic and cucumber.

3. Serve the juice alone or over ice.

PER SERVING: Calories: 81 | Fat: 1g | Protein: 5g | Sodium: 17mg | Carbohydrates: 17g | Sugar: 9g

Summer Squash Special

All the summer squashes—zucchini, yellow squash, Mexican gray squash, and patty pan squash—are excellent sources of protein, which is important to keep up during any weight loss program. Juicing is also a good way to use larger squashes because they contain much more liquid.

INGREDIENTS | YIELDS 1 CUP

1 cup spinach
1 zucchini or other summer squash
1 cucumber
2 carrots, trimmed
½ apple, cored

Other Squash Varieties

You can also choose crookneck, straight-neck, scallop squash, yellow squash, or any of the round zucchini hybrids for this recipe.

1. Process the spinach through an electronic juicer according to the manufacturer's directions.

2. Add the squash, followed by the cucumber.

3. Add the carrot and the apple.

4. Whisk the juice thoroughly to combine ingredients and enjoy!

PER SERVING: Calories: 139 | Fat: 1g | Protein: 5g | Sodium: 108mg | Carbohydrates: 32g | Sugar: 18g

Peach Cherry Shake

Be sure to use "cling free" varieties of white or yellow peaches for easier pitting and more juice.

INGREDIENTS | YIELDS 1 CUP

½ cup sweet cherries
1 orange, peeled
1 peach, pitted
1 nectarine, pitted

Popular Peaches

These fruits have been a summertime favorite ever since the Spaniards first brought them to North America. Today, California, Georgia, and South Carolina are the biggest peach producers in the United States. They are rich in niacin, vitamin C, vitamin A, and lutein.

1. Process the fruits through an electronic juicer in any order you wish.

2. Mix the juice thoroughly and drink immediately after preparation.

PER SERVING: Calories: 201 | Fat: 1g | Protein: 4g | Sodium: 0g | Carbohydrates: 49g | Sugar: 39g

Berry Refreshing

Summer is the best time of all to juice to lose weight. Not only does appetite decrease in the heat, but a huge variety of fruits and vegetables come into season, making for an abundance of great tasting, low-cal treats!

INGREDIENTS | YIELDS 1 CUP

½ cup strawberries
1 cup raspberries
1 medium orange, peeled

Raspberry Ketones

Raspberries have been shown to contain a natural substance called ketones, which are similar to capsaicin, the compound that gives hot peppers their fire. Animal studies have found that raspberry ketones prevented an increase in overall body fat and are a great metabolism booster.

1. Process the fruit in any order you wish through an electronic juicer according to the manufacturer's directions.

2. Using a cocktail shaker or covered jar, shake the juice together with some ice and enjoy!

PER SERVING: Calories: 132 | Fat: 1g | Protein: 3g | Sodium: 2mg | Carbohydrates: 31g | Sugar: 17g

Apple-Melon Cooler

Wonderfully refreshing, and fills you up, fast!

INGREDIENTS | YIELDS 1½ CUPS

2 apples, cored
3 (1-inch) slices of watermelon

1. Process the apples through an electronic juicer according to the manufacturer's directions.

2. Add the watermelon slices.

3. Serve the juice alone or over ice.

PER SERVING: Calories: 242 | Fat: 1g | Protein: 3.3g | Sodium: 4.5mg | Carbohydrates: 62g | Sugar: 50g

Green Juice

This flavorful juice is good for reducing cravings for sour foods, which can be caused by a lack of acetic acid. Green vegetables are high in chlorophyll and help with these types of cravings.

INGREDIENTS | YIELDS 1½ CUPS

3 celery stalks, leaves intact
½ cucumber
1 red apple, cored
1 cup spinach leaves
1 cup beet greens

1. Process the celery and cucumber through an electronic juicer according to the manufacturer's directions.

2. Add the apple.

3. Add the spinach and beet greens.

4. Whisk the juice to combine the ingredients, and serve alone or over ice.

PER SERVING: Calories: 132 | Fat: 0.7g | Protein: 3.7g | Sodium: 199mg | Carbohydrates: 32g | Sugar: 21g

CHAPTER 5

Juicing for Longevity and Anti-Aging

No doubt about it, people are obsessed with youth. But the desire to stay youthful isn't just about vanity, or hating those wrinkles and gray hair. If you love life, it only stands to reason that you want to extend it for as long as possible, enjoying all the benefits of good health, optimum energy, and sharpness of mind as the decades pass. Current studies indicate that people are living longer than ever before. That's partly due to advances in traditional medicine, and cures for many diseases, but it's also due to an increased public awareness of just what it takes to stay healthy and prevent disease. Good eating habits, regular exercise, and creating a healthier, more sustainable environment all play a big role in extending the life span. But whether or not you're concerned about living to be 100, it's never too soon to start taking better care of your health.

Aging Gracefully

Just how well or how fast you age can have a lot to do with genetics, but perhaps more to do with lifestyle and diet. It's a simple law of physics: Objects at rest tend to stay at rest; objects in motion tend to stay in motion. The same holds true of people. Active types tend to stay active longer, while more sedentary types are going to be less likely to motivate themselves off the couch and into a yoga class. Other factors that can affect aging include stress, environmental exposure, disease, smoking, excess alcohol, and overexposure to the sun.

Yet experts agree that the two factors critical to increased longevity and staving off some of the more unpleasant effects of Father Time are diet and exercise. And that's where juicing comes in.

Juicing and Longevity

Anyone who juices regularly is almost certainly aware of its health benefits in the areas of removing toxins, increased energy and immunity, and improving overall health. But when it comes to longevity the picture gets even brighter.

According to research compiled by the North Carolina Research Campus, the American Dietetic Association, the American Cancer Foundation, and the American Diabetes Association, there are almost as many reasons to juice for longevity and anti-aging as there are fruits and vegetables to juice with!

- Fresh juice contains proteins, carbohydrates, essential fatty acids, vitamins, and minerals in a form your body can easily absorb.
- Fresh fruit and vegetable juice is rich in potassium and low in sodium, which helps promote cardiovascular health and prevent cancer.
- The enzymes in juice are essential for digestion and the rapid absorption of nutrients in your food.
- Juice is loaded with powerful antioxidants called carotenes, found in dark leafy green vegetables and red, purple, and yellow-orange fruits and vegetables, all of which neutralize cancer-causing free radicals and promote longevity.

- The bio-availability of juice nutrition is perfect as you get older, because it's easier on the digestion. When you add juicing to your daily routine, it makes you more aware of your health choices. Increased levels of energy mean you'll be more likely to exercise and maintain muscle tone.

ESSENTIAL

There's also a subtler psychological effect that occurs when you begin to incorporate healthier habits like juicing. It's a real sign of life when you give up the notion that you're slowly falling apart. Chances are, a simple glass of fresh-pressed juice is going to help motivate you to get your act together instead!

Fresh juice also helps maintain and protect the skin, regulate metabolism, prevent high blood pressure, ease conditions such as arthritis, prevent the buildup of plaque in the arteries and adds calcium, a vital mineral for maintaining bones and teeth. This high-powered liquid nutrition also helps with hydration, which is always important, but especially so as you age. Juicing can help counter the side effects of prescription medication and even help improve memory and brain function. Further, as appetites decrease, regular juicing is a way to give the body those essential fruit and vegetable nutrients you just might not be motivated to eat otherwise. So whether you're juicing for longevity or have taken up juicing as a valuable weapon in your anti-aging arsenal, all the evidence supports that fresh juice is one sure way to live long and prosper!

Great Veggies for Longevity

According to the North Carolina Research Center, headed by the former CEO of Dole, the following are the best juicing vegetables to stay younger and healthier longer.

- **Spinach** helps with mental alertness and reduces the risk of certain cancers, including cancer of the liver, ovaries, colon, and prostate. It also contains vitamins A, B, C, D, and K.
- **Red bell peppers** help prevent sun damage, build cardiovascular health, and may decrease the risk of certain cancers, including lung, prostate, ovarian, and cervical cancer.
- **Broccoli** decreases the risk of certain cancers, including prostate, bladder, colon, pancreatic, gastric, and breast cancer; helps offset type 2 diabetes; and helps protect against brain injuries.
- **Carrots** battle cataracts and offer protection against certain cancers. They also provide vitamins A, B, and C as well as calcium, potassium, and sodium.
- **Cauliflower** helps inhibit the growth of breast cancer cells, protects against prostate cancer, and stimulates the body's detox systems. Cauliflower contains the compound allicin, which helps reduce the risk of stroke and improves heart health. Allicin also helps detoxify the blood and liver.
- **Cucumber** is rich in silica, which strengthens connective tissue of muscles, tendons, ligaments, cartilage, and bone. Cucumber juice also promotes strong, lustrous hair, glowing skin, and strong nails.
- **Artichokes** aid blood clotting and reduce bad cholesterol. Artichokes are high in vitamin C and fiber.
- **Arugula** is good for the eyes, and reduces the risk of fracture. High in beta-carotene, the antioxidant that fights heart disease, arugula is also high in vitamin C, folic acid, potassium, and fiber.
- **Asparagus** helps promote healthy bacteria in the digestive system, and builds a healthy heart. Asparagus is rich in vitamins A and B_1.
- **Green cabbage** helps with blood clotting and reduces the risk of certain cancers, including prostate, colon, breast, and ovarian cancer. Cabbage contains the nitrogenous compound indoles, which helps lower blood pressure, and has more nutrients that protect against cancer than any other vegetable. According to research conducted at Stanford University, cabbage juice can completely restore the gastrointestinal tract and heal ulcers in seven days.
- **Kale** helps regulate estrogen levels, prevent sun damage to the eyes, and build bone density.

- **Sweet potatoes** reduce the risk of stroke and cancer and offer protection against macular degeneration.
- **Mushrooms** help decrease the risk of certain cancers, including colon and prostate. They also lower blood pressure and enhance the body's natural detox systems.
- **Butternut squash** helps fight wrinkles, promote good night vision, and build a healthy heart.

Juices to Stave Off Aging

Youth Juice

This one helps restore energy and packs a real nutritional punch. The parsley not only adds necessary chlorophyll but great flavor for those who may not take to the taste of cauliflower.

INGREDIENTS | YIELDS 1 CUP

4 medium carrots, trimmed
1 cup cauliflower florets
½ cup parsley

Cauliflower Power

Cauliflower is packed with boron, which contributes to proper brain function, helps to lower cholesterol levels in the blood, helps prevent arthritis, and protects against fungal infections.

1. Process the carrots through an electronic juicer according to the manufacturer's directions.

2. Add the cauliflower florets.

3. Roll the parsley leaves into a ball to compact them, and process.

4. Whisk the ingredients thoroughly to combine and enjoy!

PER SERVING: Calories: 117 | Fat: 1g | Protein: 4.5g | Sodium: 184mg | Carbohydrates: 26g | Sugar: 11g

Apple Celery Cucumber Cocktail

Take this one at bedtime to ease inflammation, prevent stiff joints, and promote a good night's sleep.

INGREDIENTS | YIELDS 2 CUPS (2 SERVINGS)

2 medium apples, cored
4 stalks celery, with leaves
1 cucumber, cut into chunks

Make the Connection

Cucumber juice is rich in silica, which strengthens connective tissue of muscles, tendons, ligaments, cartilage, and bone.

1. Slice the apples and process through the feed tube of an electronic juicer according to the manufacturer's directions.

2. Add the celery stalks, one or two at a time.

3. Add the cucumber chunks.

4. Whisk the juice together to blend and serve immediately.

PER SERVING: Calories: 168 | Fat: 1g | Protein: 3.3g | Sodium: 95mg | Carbohydrates: 42g | Sugar: 29g

Pepper UP!

Bell peppers come in an array of colors: red, green, yellow, orange, and even purple! Each contains different levels of the pepper's basic nutrients, so mix it up and enjoy!

INGREDIENTS | YIELDS 1 CUP

½ red bell pepper, cored and seeded
½ green bell pepper, cored and seeded
½ yellow bell pepper, cored and seeded
3 tomatoes
2 stalks celery, with leaves
½ cup parsley
½ lemon, peeled

Ring the Bell

Bell peppers are packed with vitamin C and contain other nutrients that have been shown to be essential in preventing heart attacks and stroke.

1. Process the pepper sections through an electronic juicer according to the manufacturer's directions.

2. Add the tomatoes, followed by the celery.

3. Roll the parsley into a ball to compress and add to the juicer, followed by the lemon.

4. Whisk the juice to combine and serve in a chilled glass or over ice.

PER SERVING: Calories: 140 | Fat: 1.5g | Protein: 6.6g | Sodium: 105mg | Carbohydrates: 30g | Sugar: 17g

The Eyes Have It

When carrots are eaten raw, you only absorb 1 percent of the carrot's available beta-carotene. When you juice your carrots, that amount is increased by almost a hundredfold. Plus, the sweet potato included in this recipe is rich in vitamin B_6, which has been shown to be essential in the maintenance of healthy blood vessels.

INGREDIENTS | YIELDS 1½ CUPS

4 medium carrots, trimmed

1 sweet potato, peeled

1 cup pineapple chunks

2 medium oranges, peeled

Feeling Ravaged by Time?

The nutrients in fresh fruit and vegetable juice are also responsible for reducing or eliminating high cholesterol, carpal tunnel, constipation, gallstones, glaucoma, hypertension, indigestion, insomnia, kidney stones, macular degeneration, menopause, osteoporosis, prostate enlargement, psoriasis, and varicose veins.

1. Process the carrots, one at a time, through an electronic juicer according to the manufacturer's directions.

2. Cut the sweet potato into chunks and add to the juicer.

3. Add the pineapple chunks, followed by the orange segments.

4. Whisk the juice together to combine and serve immediately.

PER SERVING: Calories: 366 | Fat: 1g | Protein: 6.5g | Sodium: 211mg | Carbohydrates: 89g | Sugar: 49g

Super Carotene Combo

Carotene is especially helpful for the eyes but also helps the liver. In addition to providing a great energy boost, it's also believed to be especially helpful in preventing the onset of type 2 diabetes.

INGREDIENTS | YIELDS 1½ CUPS

3 medium carrots, trimmed

½ large cantaloupe, peeled and seeded

1 medium sweet potato, peeled and cut into chunks

1 tablespoon fresh mint leaves

Mint and Melon

The classic combination of flavors is the perfect summertime refreshment. Not only do fresh mint leaves add wonderful flavor, they add chlorophyll and a touch of green goodness to this bright orange juice. Garnish with additional mint leaves for extra eye appeal.

1. Process the carrots through an electronic juicer according to the manufacturer's directions.

2. Cut the cantaloupe into chunks and add.

3. Add the sweet potato.

4. Roll the mint leaves into a ball to compress and add to the juicer.

5. Whisk the juice together and serve over ice, if desired.

PER SERVING: Calories: 250 | Fat: 0.8g | Protein: 5.5g | Sodium: 211mg | Carbohydrates: 58g | Sugar: 29g

Fabulous Fig Smoothie

If you're fortunate enough to have fresh figs, you already know how delightful they can be. If you have a masticating juicer, use a wider mesh net attachment to allow some fiber to pass through. Alternatively, for a thicker smoothie texture, process the figs in a blender to purée, then add to the juice.

INGREDIENTS | YIELDS 1½ CUPS

10 figs, halved

3 medium carrots, trimmed

1 small sugar beet, greens optional

2 stalks celery, with leaves

2 medium apples, cored

1 cucumber, sliced

½ lemon, peeled

1. Process the figs in a masticating juicer or blender until smooth.

2. Process the carrots and beets through an electronic juicer according to the manufacturer's directions.

3. Add the celery, apples, and cucumber to the juicer, followed by the lemon.

4. Whisk or blend the ingredients together and enjoy!

PER SERVING: Calories: 613 | Fat: 2.5g | Protein: 9.5g | Sodium: 242mg | Fiber: 25g | Carbohydrates: 156g | Sugar: 117g

Health Benefits of Figs

Figs are high in potassium, important for lowering high blood pressure (hypertension) and controlling blood sugar levels in diabetics.

Health Harvest Special

In late summer and early autumn, it's hard to come home from the farmers' market without feeling that you've just bought more than you could ever eat! Juicing is a great way to manage Nature's bounty and take advantage of all the goodness the season provides!

INGREDIENTS | YIELDS 1½ CUPS

1 small sugar beet, greens optional
6 carrots, trimmed
2 stalks celery, with leaves
1 cucumber
1 grapefruit, peeled
1 kiwi fruit
1 red or black plum, pitted
2 Bosch or Anjou pears, cored
2 apples, cored

1. Process the beets and carrots through an electronic juicer according to the manufacturer's directions.

2. Add the celery and cucumber.

3. Add the grapefruit sections, followed by the kiwi.

4. Add the plum and the pears, followed by the apple.

5. Whisk or shake the juice to combine and serve over ice, if desired.

PER SERVING: Calories: 634 | Fat: 2.5g | Protein: 11g | Sodium: 347mg | Carbohydrates: 158g | Sugar: 97g

Green Goddess

If the flavor of this kale-based juice seems too intense, add distilled water or half a container of plain yogurt.

INGREDIENTS | YIELDS 1 CUP

2 medium apples, cored
2 medium carrots, trimmed
2 medium pears, cored
½ cucumber
6–8 leaves fresh kale

1. Process the apples and carrots through an electronic juicer according to the manufacturer's directions.

2. Add the pears, followed by the cucumber.

3. Roll the kale leaves together to compress and add to the juicer.

4. Stir or shake the mixture to combine ingredients.

PER SERVING: Calories: 474 | Fat: 3g | Protein: 12.5g | Sodium: 190mg | Carbohydrates: 115g | Sugar: 58g

The Anti-Aging Body Booster

*Cherries contain lutein. Lutein plus vitamins A and C up collagen production,
which results in stronger bones and younger-looking skin.*

INGREDIENTS | YIELDS 1½ CUPS

1 medium apple, cored

2 medium pears, cored

½ cup Bing or Queen Anne cherries, pitted

Antioxidants Anyone?

Cherries are extraordinarily high in the nutrients necessary to help the body destroy free radicals. Data from the USDA's 2007 Oxygen Radical Absorbance Capacity table gives sweet cherries a total ORAC score of 3,365 per 3.5 ounces.

1. Process the apple through an electronic juicer according to the manufacturer's directions.

2. Add the pears, followed by the cherries.

3. Whisk the juice to combine ingredients and enjoy!

PER SERVING: Calories: 332 | Fat: 0.7g | Protein: 2.6g | Sodium: 3.5mg | Carbohydrates: 87g | Sugar: 61g

Cucumber Pear Plus!

*The plus in this recipe comes from sugar snap peas, a rich source of folates.
Snap peas have 150 percent more vitamin C than regular garden peas and also contain
phytosterols, which help lower cholesterol.*

INGREDIENTS | YIELDS 1½ CUPS

3 medium pears, cored

1 medium cucumber, peeled

2 cups spinach

6 leaves kale

½ leaf Swiss chard

½ lemon, peeled

1 cup sugar snap peas

Snap!

Sugar snap peas also are a good source of riboflavin, vitamin B_6, pantothenic acid, magnesium, phosphorus, and potassium, in addition to fiber, vitamin A, vitamin K, thiamin, iron, and manganese.

1. Process the pears through an electronic juicer according to the manufacturer's directions.

2. Add the cucumber, followed by the spinach.

3. Roll the kale and chard leaves together to compress and add to the juicer.

4. Add the lemon and the snap peas.

5. Whisk the juice to combine the ingredients and serve immediately.

PER SERVING: Calories: 422 | Fat: 2g | Protein: 12g | Sodium: 169mg | Carbohydrates: 103g | Sugar: 52g

Grapeberry Cocktail

Grapes are rich in the phytochemical resveratrol, a powerful antioxidant, that has been found to play a protective role against cancers of colon and prostate, heart disease, degenerative nerve disease, Alzheimer's, and viral/ fungal infections. Not only that, it has marvelous benefits for aging skin and is a key ingredient in many anti-aging cosmetics.

INGREDIENTS | YIELDS 1 CUP

3 cups Concord grapes

1 medium apple, cored

½ cup blackberries

All about Blackberries

Blackberries help to lower your risk of heart disease and stroke, and they may lower your risk of certain cancers. Blackberries may also help to prevent diabetes and age-related cognitive decline. When choosing blackberries, be sure they don't have the hulls or green leaves attached. If they do, it means they were picked too early and they will not ripen after they have been picked.

1. Process the grapes through an electronic juicer according to the manufacturer's directions.

2. Add the apple, followed by the blackberries.

3. Mix the juice thoroughly and enjoy!

PER SERVING: Calories: 420 | Fat: 1.2g | Protein: 4.5g | Sodium: 10mg | Carbohydrates: 109g | Sugar: 89g

Cranberry Citrus Punch

*If this one's too tart for your taste buds, try sweetening it
with a little raw honey.*

INGREDIENTS | YIELDS 1½ CUPS

3 cups cranberries, fresh or frozen

3 oranges, peeled

2 pink grapefruits, peeled

2 limes, peeled

Cranberry Facts

Cranberries contain some specific phyto-nutrients that just can't be found any-where else. Plus, researchers have discovered that isolated phytonutrients in cranberries do not account for the same degree of health benefit as the same phytonutrients taken as a group. What it means is that the whole cranberry best supports your health, especially the urinary tract, as an anti-inflammatory and for help in the prevention of kidney and gallstones.

1. Process the cranberries through an electronic juicer according to the manufacturer's directions.

2. Add the orange sections, followed by the grapefruits and limes.

3. Mix the juice thoroughly and enjoy over ice if desired.

PER SERVING: Calories: 441 | Fat: 1.5g | Protein: 7g | Sodium: 9mg | Carbohydrates: 116g | Sugar: 69g

Memory Enhancer

Zinc has been shown by numerous studies to improve memory. The cauliflower in this juice provides zinc, and the vitamin E found in the tomatoes protects your cell membranes.

INGREDIENTS | YIELDS 1 CUP

1 tomato

3 red lettuce leaves

½ cup cauliflower

How to Wash Lettuce

Wash and drain lettuce very well. You should blot the lettuce with a towel to ensure that you have removed all of the excess moisture. Do not soak lettuce. This will make the leaves soft. Even if you buy organic lettuce, it is important to rinse it before eating it.

1. Process the tomato through an electronic juicer according to the manufacturer's directions.

2. Add the lettuce and cauliflower.

3. Mix the juice thoroughly and enjoy over ice if desired.

PER SERVING: Calories: 56 | Fat: 0.6g | Protein: 3.5g | Sodium: 44mg | Carbohydrates: 11.5g | Sugar: 6g

Fountain of Youth Cocktail

This refreshing anti-aging juice is packed with vitamins and antioxidants.
Start your morning with all the nutritious benefits this juice has to offer.

INGREDIENTS | YIELDS ¾ CUP

1 pint blackberries
1 pint raspberries
½ lemon, peeled
1 (¼-inch) piece fresh ginger

What Are Antioxidants?

Antioxidants are nutrients that can prevent or slow the oxidative damage to your body. When your body's cells use oxygen, they naturally produce free radicals that can cause damage. Antioxidants work as scavengers, gobbling up the free radicals and preventing and repairing the damage they cause.

1. Process the berries through an electronic juicer according to the manufacturer's directions.

2. Add the lemon and ginger.

3. Mix the juice thoroughly and enjoy over ice if desired.

PER SERVING: Calories: 261 | Fat: 3g | Protein: 7g | Sodium: 6mg | Carbohydrates: 60g | Sugar: 25g

Easy Greens

Romaine lettuce is great for juicing because it tends to be more substantial than some other lettuces and therefore yields more juice! If greens are just not your thing, this one's great because it has a light, easy flavor with no cabbage-y tasting undertone.

INGREDIENTS | YIELDS 1½ CUPS

2 hearts of romaine lettuce
1 bunch arugula, about 1 cup
½ cup spinach
1 bunch parsley
3 stalks celery, with leaves
½ lemon, peeled

1. Process the romaine hearts through an electronic juicer according to the manufacturer's directions.

2. Add the arugula, followed by the spinach and the parsley.

3. Add the celery and the lemon.

4. Mix the juice thoroughly and enjoy over ice, if desired.

PER SERVING: Calories: 63 | Fat: 1g | Protein: 4.3g | Sodium: 150mg | Carbohydrates: 12g | Sugar: 4g

Terrific Turnip Juice

Like many root vegetables, turnips can be a bit earthy tasting, but inclusion of the fennel bulb in this concoction imparts a wonderful flavor!

INGREDIENTS | YIELDS 1 CUP

½ turnip, peeled
3 carrots, trimmed
1 apple, cored
¼ fennel bulb

Fabulous Fennel

In addition to wonderful flavor, fennel is a good source of niacin, calcium, iron, magnesium, phosphorus, and copper, and also contains vitamin C, folate, potassium, and manganese.

1. Process the turnip and carrots through an electronic juicer according to the manufacturer's directions.

2. Add the apple and the fennel bulb.

3. Mix the juice thoroughly to blend and serve over ice.

PER SERVING: Calories: 165 | Fat: 0.7g | Protein: 2.8g | Sodium: 154mg | Carbohydrates: 41g | Sugar: 24g

Magic Parsley Potion

Magic? Well almost. Parsley is so rich in chlorophyll and phytonutrients, one juice aficionado claims it's a true natural high, because it imparts such a boost of energy.

INGREDIENTS | YIELDS 1 CUP

1 bunch flat leaf Italian parsley
2 carrots, trimmed
1 apple, cored
2 stalks celery, with leaves

1. Compress the parsley by rolling it into a ball. Process through an electronic juicer according to the manufacturer's directions.

2. Add the carrots and the apple, followed by the celery.

3. Mix the juice thoroughly to blend and serve over ice.

PER SERVING: Calories: 138 | Fat: 1g | Protein: 3.6g | Sodium: 166mg | Carbohydrates: 32g | Sugar: 20g

Tangerine Tango

It's called the tango because it only takes two—tangerines and oranges—to make this spectacular juice.

INGREDIENTS | YIELDS 1 CUP

2 to 3 tangerines, peeled
1 large orange, peeled

Tangerine Temptation

Tangerines are in the mandarin family. They're easy to peel, wonderfully sweet, and highly nutritious. People who have a difficult time digesting oranges can find tangerines easier on the system, too. One small tangerine can have more vitamin C than a large orange, and they help to prevent heart disease, are anti-inflammatory, improve eyesight, help relieve arthritis, and can be an aid in preventing certain cancers such as breast cancer and melanoma.

1. Process the fruits through an electronic juicer according to the manufacturer's directions.

2. Serve immediately.

PER SERVING: Calories: 125 | Fat: 0.5g | Protein: 2g | Sodium: 3mg | Carbohydrates: 31g | Sugar: 25g

Insomnia Cure

Going through a rough time? Carrots, zucchini, cabbage, and ginger all contain nutrients that help to alleviate anxiety, a major cause of troubled sleep.

INGREDIENTS | YIELDS 2 CUPS (2 SERVINGS)

3 carrots, trimmed

1 apple, cored

1 whole head romaine lettuce

1 cup broccoli florets

1 zucchini

½ head green cabbage

1 (1-inch) piece fresh ginger

Catching your ZZZZZs

As they age, most people will be inclined to fall asleep earlier and wake up earlier. However, most cases of insomnia are caused by underlying treatable causes. Stress, anxiety, and depression can cause insomnia, but the most common causes in seniors are a poor sleep environment or poor daytime habits.

1. Process the carrots and the apple through an electronic juicer according to the manufacturer's directions.

2. Add the lettuce a few leaves at a time, followed by broccoli.

3. Add the zucchini, followed by the cabbage and the ginger.

4. Mix the juice thoroughly to combine ingredients and drink immediately before bedtime.

PER SERVING: Calories: 402 | Fat: 3.6g | Protein: 19g | Sodium: 275mg | Carbohydrates: 89g | Sugar: 46g

Breathe Easy

This recipe is especially good for older adults afflicted with COPD, allergies, or asthma. It also has the added benefit of aiding eyesight.

INGREDIENTS | YIELDS 1 CUP

2 cups broccoli florets
1 large cucumber
1 medium zucchini
10 stalks asparagus, trimmed

1. Process the broccoli through an electronic juicer according to the manufacturer's directions.

2. Add the cucumber.

3. Add the zucchini, followed by the asparagus.

4. Mix the juice thoroughly to combine ingredients and drink immediately.

PER SERVING: Calories: 118 | Fat: 1.2g | Protein: 9.7g | Sodium: 73mg | Carbohydrates: 23g | Sugar: 9.7g

Libido Lifter

Great for getting back some of the old spark, this juice is best prepared in a blender or bullet-type juicer.

INGREDIENTS | YIELDS 2½ CUPS (2 SERVINGS)

2 stalks celery, with leaves
½ banana, frozen
1 (½ inch) piece fresh ginger
½ avocado, peeled and pitted
½ cup basil leaves
3 fresh figs
2 cups coconut water

Place all ingredients in the work bowl of a blender or bullet-type juicer and purée until smooth.

PER SERVING: Calories: 160 | Fat: 7.8g | Protein: 2.5g | Sodium: 37mg | Fiber: 6.7 | Carbohydrates: 23g | Sugar: 13g

Getting Fresh

When fresh figs aren't available, reconstitute dried figs in plain water or coconut water until soft.

Spinach Cantaloupe Cocktail

In a recent study, spinach showed evidence of significant protection against the occurrence of aggressive prostate cancer—more reason to eat this beneficial green.

INGREDIENTS | YIELDS 1 CUP

1 cup spinach
2 medium carrots, trimmed
1 cup cantaloupe chunks

1. Process the spinach through an electronic juicer according to the manufacturer's directions.

2. Add the carrots, followed by the cantaloupe.

3. Stir or shake the juice to combine the ingredients and serve.

PER SERVING: Calories: 109 | Fat: 0.7g | Protein: 3.3g | Sodium: 132mg | Carbohydrates: 25g | Sugar: 18g

Blue Hawaii

Try this in your fight against Father Time. The super combination of blueberries and pineapple will make you feel like a kid again!

INGREDIENTS | YIELDS 1 CUP

¼ pineapple, peeled
1 cup blueberries
1 (½-inch) piece fresh ginger

1. Process the pineapple and blueberries through an electronic juicer according to the manufacturer's directions.

2. Add the ginger.

3. Whisk the juice to combine the ingredients and serve over ice.

PER SERVING: Calories: 216 | Fat: 1g | Protein: 3g | Sodium: 5mg | Carbohydrates: 54g | Sugar: 37g

Hot Tomato

The pungent addition of horseradish to this recipe doesn't just add flavor; horseradish is anti-inflammatory, antioxidant, and has been found to have soothing effects on the nerves.

INGREDIENTS | YIELDS 1½ CUPS

1 cup red or yellow cherry tomatoes

1 large carrot, trimmed

1 stalk celery, with leaves

1 (1-inch) piece fresh ginger

1 (1-inch) piece horseradish root

¼ lemon, peeled

3 or 4 sprigs fresh cilantro

1 radish

1 clove garlic, peeled

1. Process the tomatoes through an electronic juicer according to the manufacturer's directions.

2. Add the carrot, followed by the celery.

3. Add the ginger, horseradish, and lemon.

4. Add the cilantro, the radish, and the garlic.

5. Mix the juice thoroughly to combine ingredients and serve over ice.

PER SERVING: Calories: 99 | Fat: 1g | Protein: 3.5g | Sodium: 143mg | Carbohydrates: 22g | Sugar: 9g

Yellow Tomatoes

The only significant nutritional difference between red tomatoes and yellow is that the yellow varieties tend to be somewhat lower in acids, so if you have a sensitive stomach, they're a good choice.

Sweet Tart

Pears provide a nice balance to the tart grapefruit in this juice.

INGREDIENTS | YIELDS 1 CUP

1 large pink grapefruit, peeled
2 Anjou pears, cored

Pear ABCs

When it comes to pick perfect pears, remember they ripen off the tree, so if you don't plan to use them right away, there's no harm in buying them rock hard. The best pears for juicing are simple as ABC: Anjou, Bartlett, and Comice.

1. Process the grapefruit and pears through an electronic juicer according to the manufacturer's directions.

2. Whisk the juice to combine the ingredients and serve over ice.

PER SERVING: Calories: 235 | Fat: 0.5g | Protein: 2.3g | Sodium: 3mg | Carbohydrates: 61g | Sugar: 42g

Citrus Surprise (Chapter 9)

Minty Refresher (Chapter 4)

Orange Bonanza (Chapter 4)

Cranberry Citrus Punch (Chapter 5)

Vegetable Super Juice (Chapter 2)

Chocolate Banana Shake (Chapter 13)

Libido Lifter (Chapter 5)

Orange Strawberry Banana Juice (Chapter 2)

Strawberry Tomato Temptation (Chapter 4)

Carrot Mango Cup (Chapter 7)

Apple Celery Cucumber Cocktail (Chapter 5)

Glamorous Greens (Chapter 3)

Relaxing Cooler (Chapter 2)

Liquid Cruciferous (Chapter 4)

Bedtime Snack (Chapter 10)

Carrot Cleanse (Chapter 3)

Sweet Shake (Chapter 4)

The Detox Special (Chapter 3)

Blueberry-Banana Smoothie (Chapter 13)

Spinach Cantaloupe Cocktail (Chapter 5)

Super Weight Loss Cocktail (Chapter 4)

Blue Hawaii (Chapter 5)

Green Slime Super Juice (Chapter 10)

Pumpkin Pie Smoothie (Chapter 13)

CHAPTER 6

Juicing for Beautiful Hair, Skin, and Nails

Every year, people spend a fortune trying to achieve three things: a glowing complexion; thick, shiny hair; and strong, beautiful nails. But the real secret to getting, and maintaining, these things is nutrition. If you're dropping big bucks on creams for your skin, pricy hair products, and weekly manicures, you're missing out on the most effective way to ensure you look great—juicing! Beauty may be only skin deep, but it begins on the inside—with a healthy diet of fruits and vegetables that provide your skin, hair, and nails with the nutrients they need.

Keratin

The fact is, your skin, hair, and nails are some of the most powerful indicators of your overall health. That's because they have a common building block, a protein called keratin. As keratin cells naturally push upward through the skin, they die and then harden, turning into your hair and nails, or are "shed" as the skin cells are replaced. Healthy bodies will produce smooth nails without ridges; thick, strong hair that isn't prone to falling out or breakage; and a clear glowing complexion, while problems in these areas can be a signal from your body that you're not getting the nutrients you need.

Consider also that so many skin care manufacturers are turning to Nature's medicine chest and substituting vitamins, natural oils, fruit acids, and nutrients in topical cosmetics. Good as those aids may be, it only makes sense to begin your beauty regime from the inside out.

What to Eat for Your Skin, Hair, and Nails

Here are some of the most important nutrients for a glowing complexion, beautiful hair, and strong, healthy nails:

- **Selenium** plays a key role in skin cancer prevention and protects skin from sun damage. If you're a sun worshipper, selenium could help reduce your chance of burning. Pumpkins are a good source of selenium.
- **Silica** is a trace mineral that strengthens the body's connective tissues and is found in cucumbers. Too little silica can result in reduced skin elasticity and slower healing of wounds.
- **Zinc** controls the production of oil in the skin and may also help control some of the hormones that create acne. It clears skin by taming oil production and controlling the formation of acne lesions and is found in spinach, grapes, and garlic.
- **Calcium** strengthens not just nails but bones and connective tissues as well. Oranges and tangerines are rich in calcium.
- **Essential fatty acids**, also called omega acids, moisturize and maintain the skin's flexibility. Without enough of them, the skin produces a more irritating form of sebum, or oil, which dries the skin and clogs

pores, causing acne and inflammation. Avocados are a rich source of these nutrients.

- **Vitamin C** reduces damage caused by free radicals, a harmful byproduct of sunlight, smoke, and pollution that destroys collagen and elastin (fibers that support your skin structure) and results in wrinkles and other signs of aging. Citrus fruits are a well-known source of vitamin C as are many other fruits and vegetables.

- **Vitamin E** helps reduce sun damage, wrinkles, and uneven textures caused by sun damage. Strawberries and lettuce both contain vitamin E.

- **Vitamin B** complex, especially biotin, is the nutrient that forms the basis of skin, nail, and hair cells. Without enough B vitamins, dermatitis and hair loss can occur. Apples, Swiss chard, and papaya are all excellent sources of B-complex vitamins.

- **Vitamin A** is necessary for the maintenance and repair of skin tissue. Look for it in raspberries, kale, and cherries.

Juices for Improving Your Outside

Silky Skin

Pineapple has long been known for its benefits to the skin.
Add the silica-rich cucumber, and you've got an unbeatable combination.

INGREDIENTS | YIELDS 1 CUP

1 cup peeled pineapple chunks
1 mango, pitted
1 cucumber
½ lemon, rind intact, thinly sliced

Pineapple Benefits for Skin

Pineapple contains enzymes that improve skin's elasticity. It also improves skin hydration, and speeds up the process that removes damaged and dead cells. In addition, the enzymes in pineapples fight free-radical damage and can reduce age spots and fine lines.

1. Process the pineapple through an electronic juicer according to the manufacturer's directions.

2. Add the mango and the cucumber.

3. Add the lemon.

4. Stir or shake the juice well to combine ingredients and enjoy!

PER SERVING: Calories: 270 | Fat: 1g | Protein: 4g | Sodium: 12mg | Carbohydrates: 70g | Sugar: 52g

Apple Grape Cocktail

Many lines of creams and cosmetics are using grapeseed oils and extracts for their benefits to the skin,
so if you happen to have seeded grapes on hand, don't hesitate to use them!

INGREDIENTS | YIELDS 1 CUP

2 red Gala or Fuji apples, cored
1 cup grapes, any variety

1. Process the apples through your electronic juicer according to the manufacturer's directions.

2. Add the grapes.

3. Mix the juice thoroughly to combine and serve alone or over ice.

PER SERVING: Calories: 209 | Fat: 0.5g | Protein: 1.5g | Sodium: 3mg | Carbohydrates: 55g | Sugar: 45g

Apple Strawberry Temptation

Strawberries are known for their abilities to fight free radicals and the environmental damage that comes from pollutants in the air and water.

INGREDIENTS | YIELDS 1½ CUPS

2 Gala apples, cored
2 Granny Smith apples, cored
1 cup strawberries
¼ lemon, rind intact

1. Process the apples through your electronic juicer according to the manufacturer's directions.

2. Add the strawberries, followed by the lemon wedge.

3. Mix the juice thoroughly to combine and serve alone or over ice.

PER SERVING: Calories: 204 | Fat: 0.8g | Protein: 2g | Sodium: 1.7mg | Carbohydrates: 53g | Sugar: 39g

Cucumber Complexion Tonic

Cucumbers are known to help the skin from becoming overly dry. Cucumbers contain silica, which helps improve the complexion.

INGREDIENTS | YIELDS 1¼ CUPS

½ large cucumber, peeled
1 celery stalk, leaves intact
2 sprigs fresh baby dill, for garnish

1. Process the cucumber through your electronic juicer according to the manufacturer's directions.

2. Add the celery.

3. Mix the juice thoroughly to combine and add fresh sprigs of dill to the top of the drink for garnish.

PER SERVING: Calories: 13 | Fat: 0g | Protein: 0.5g | Sodium: 33mg | Carbohydrates: 2.7g | Sugar: 1.4g

Pineapple Papaya Potion

For a delicious complexion, use the leftover fruit pulp from this juice as a face mask.
Leave it on for 10 minutes, or until slightly sticky, rinse well, and pat dry.

INGREDIENTS | YIELDS 1 CUP

1 cup pineapple, peeled
½ cup strawberries
½ papaya, seeds removed

Papaya

Papaya contains many of the same enzymes found in pineapple, and hold many of the same benefits for the skin, so this recipe packs a double punch!

1. Process the pineapple chunks through your electronic juicer according to the manufacturer's directions,.

2. Add the strawberries.

3. Add the papaya.

4. Stir or shake the juice thoroughly to combine and serve alone or over ice.

PER SERVING: Calories: 135 | Fat: 0.5g | Protein: 1.8g | Sodium: 4.6mg | Carbohydrates: 34g | Sugar: 24g

Acne Blaster

Whether you're troubled by long-term acne problems or annoying little monthly breakouts,
this one will help clear your skin fast!

INGREDIENTS | YIELDS 1 CUP

2 medium carrots, trimmed
1 medium cucumber
1 cup spinach

Spinach and Memory

A recent study showed that when elderly people ate spinach, it prevented memory loss and even reversed it, so don't forget to eat your spinach!

1. Process the carrots through your electronic juicer according to the manufacturer's directions.

2. Add the cucumber, followed by the spinach.

3. Stir or shake the juice thoroughly to combine and serve alone or over ice.

PER SERVING: Calories: 102 | Fat: 0.7g | Protein: 4g | Sodium: 113mg | Carbohydrates: 23g | Sugar: 10g

Clear Complexion Cocktail

This drink will help keep your skin clear of acne. Reducing junk foods and drinking healthy juice will be a step in the right direction, too.

INGREDIENTS | YIELDS 1¼ CUPS

2 red apples, cored
2 carrots, peeled
4 large kale leaves
1 cup spinach leaves

Let's Take Some E

According to *The Journal of Investigative Dermatology*, people who consumed vitamins C and E saw a reduction in sunburns caused by exposure to UVB radiation, as well as a reduction of factors linked to DNA damage within skin cells. Scientists believe these two antioxidant vitamins may help protect against DNA damage.

1. Process the apples through your electronic juicer according to the manufacturer's directions, followed by the carrots.

2. Add the kale and spinach.

3. Stir or shake the juice thoroughly to combine and serve alone or over ice.

PER SERVING: Calories: 208 | Fat: 1g | Protein: 5g | Sodium: 121mg | Carbohydrates: 51g | Sugar: 31g

Cactus Juice

The aloe vera plant is widely known for its topical benefits for the skin, but it has internal benefits as well. Egyptian papyrus writings told of Egyptian queens who associated aloe with their physical beauty, while Greek and Roman doctors routinely used it in their practices to heal a wide range of ailments.

INGREDIENTS | YIELDS 1 CUP

2 large fronds aloe vera
2 prickly pears, spines removed
1 orange, peeled

More about Aloe

Choose the largest fronds available when juicing aloe and be sure to consume your juice immediately. Even when stabilized by additional vitamin C as in the recipe here, it will go rancid fast. Dog owners should also use caution, as the plant can be toxic for dogs.

1. Process the aloe through your electronic juicer according to the manufacturer's directions.

2. Add the prickly pears.

3. Add the orange segments.

4. Stir or shake the juice thoroughly to combine and serve immediately.

PER SERVING: Calories: 198 | Fat: 1g | Protein: 3g | Sodium: 18mg | Carbohydrates: 41g | Sugar: 6g

Prickly Pear Cocktail

Prickly pears are also known as cactus pears. These small, egg-shaped fruits contain edible seeds and are rich in a wide variety of phytonutrients and vitamin C. Be sure to peel your pears before you use them as the rind is not digestible.

INGREDIENTS | YIELDS 1 CUP

2 prickly pears, peeled

3 medium carrots, trimmed

1 cup red grapes

Beautiful Beta-Carotene

Vitamin A in the form of beta-carotene is a pigment that protects the health of your eyes and skin.

1. Process the prickly pears through your electronic juicer according to the manufacturer's directions.

2. Add the carrots, followed by the grapes.

3. Stir or shake the juice thoroughly to combine and serve immediately.

PER SERVING: Calories: 250 | Fat: 1.5g | Protein: 4g | Sodium: 116mg | Carbohydrates: 61g | Sugar: 30g

Raspberry Peach Passion

So good tasting, you'll want some every day! Passion fruit is rich in fiber, potassium, and vitamins A and C.

INGREDIENTS | YIELDS 1½ CUPS

2 large peaches, pitted
1 cup raspberries
1 cup passion fruit pulp

A Passion for Passion Fruit

Choose fruits that are well ripened, plump, and heavy for their size. Fruits with a lightly wrinkled skin are actually more flavorful. Scoop out the pulp and discard the tough shell.

1. Process the peaches through your electronic juicer according to the manufacturer's directions.

2. Add the raspberries, followed by the passion fruit.

3. Stir or shake the juice thoroughly to combine ingredients and serve over ice.

PER SERVING: Calories: 329 | Fat: 2g | Protein: 9g | Sodium: 67mg | Carbohydrates: 93g | Sugar: 51g

Peach Perfection

Peaches are a wonderful source of vitamin E, which is especially beneficial for the skin.

INGREDIENTS | YIELDS 1 CUP

2 peaches, pitted
2 apricots, pitted
½ cup green grapes

All about Apricots

These much-prized fruits were first brought to Europe by Greeks, who called them "golden eggs of the sun." Sun-dried organic fruits have more concentrated nutrient values than fresh ones, although they have less vitamin C content.

1. Process the peaches through your electronic juicer according to the manufacturer's directions.

2. Add the apricots, followed by the grapes.

3. Stir or shake the juice thoroughly to combine the ingredients and serve.

PER SERVING: Calories: 187 | Fat: 1g | Protein: 3.8g | Sodium: 2mg | Carbohydrates: 46g | Sugar: 39g

Nectarine Cooler

Like its close cousin the peach, nectarines originated in China from where they spread to central Asia, Persia, and Europe through ancient silk routes.

INGREDIENTS | YIELDS 1 CUP

4 nectarines, pitted
1 carrot, trimmed
1 orange, peeled

1. Process the nectarines through your electronic juicer according to the manufacturer's directions.

2. Add the carrot, followed by the orange segments.

3. Stir or shake the juice thoroughly to combine the ingredients and serve.

PER SERVING: Calories: 318 | Fat: 1.9g | Protein: 7g | Sodium: 49mg | Carbohydrates: 76g | Sugar: 56g

Tropical Cucumber

This drink provides skin benefits. Cucumber contains silica, a trace mineral that helps provide strength to the connective tissues of the skin. Cucumbers help with swelling of the eyes and water retention. They are high in vitamins A and C and folic acid.

INGREDIENTS | YIELDS 2 CUPS

1 cup pineapple, peeled, cored, and cut into chunks
1 mango, pitted
1 cucumber, peeled
½ lemon, rind intact

1. Process the pineapple through your electronic juicer according to the manufacturer's directions.

2. Add the mango, followed by the cucumber.

3. Cut lemon into thin slices and add it last.

4. Stir the juice well before serving.

PER SERVING: Calories: 270 | Fat: 1g | Protein: 4g | Sodium: 12mg | Carbohydrates: 70g | Sugar: 52g

Green Glow

No, it won't make you glow green,
but it will give your skin and hair a marvelously healthy new look.

INGREDIENTS | YIELDS 1½ CUPS

1 head romaine lettuce
5 leaves of kale
2 pears, cored
1 lemon peeled, cut into quarters

More about Kale

Kale is very rich in vitamin A, which not only fights cancer but also is required for maintaining healthy mucus membranes and skin.

1. Process the lettuce through your electronic juicer according to the manufacturer's directions.

2. Add the kale, followed by the pears and lemon.

3. Stir or shake the juice thoroughly to combine ingredients and serve.

PER SERVING: Calories: 328 | Fat: 2.8g | Protein: 11g | Sodium: 83mg | Carbohydrates: 78g | Sugar: 37g

Red, White, and Blue

Great for looking gorgeous in short order! Red and blue berries combine with
white-fleshed apple to make a great-tasting combination for looking good.

INGREDIENTS | YIELDS 1½ CUPS

2 cups strawberries
2 cups blueberries
1½ cups raspberries
1 apple, cored

1. Process the berries through an electronic juicer according to the manufacturer's directions.

2. Add the apple.

3. Stir or shake the juice to combine ingredients and enjoy!

PER SERVING: Calories: 420 | Fat: 3g | Protein: 6.6g | Sodium: 7mg | Carbohydrates: 103g | Sugar: 65g

Dilled Cucumber Cocktail

Try this juice for a gorgeous mane and a magnificent manicure. It tastes great, too.

INGREDIENTS | YIELDS 1 CUP

1 large cucumber
5 or 6 stalks asparagus
½ bunch fresh dill

Delicious Dill

Not just for pickles, dill is related to the cilantro family and contains many essential volatile oils such as d-carvone, dillapiol, DHC, eugenol, limonene, terpinene, and myristicin.

1. Process the cucumber through an electronic juicer according to the manufacturer's directions.

2. Add the asparagus, followed by the dill.

3. Whisk the juice to combine the ingredients and serve over ice.

PER SERVING: Calories: 30 | Fat: 0.2g | Protein: 2.4g | Sodium: 6mg | Carbohydrates: 6.5g | Sugar: 3g

Plum Delicious

This juice is rich in selenium, silica, and resveratrol—all essentials for beautiful skin.

INGREDIENTS | YIELDS 1½ CUPS

2 cups red seedless grapes
2 red or black plums, pitted
½ large cucumber

1. Process the grapes through an electronic juicer according to the manufacturer's directions.

2. Add the plums, followed by the cucumber.

3. Stir or shake the juice to combine ingredients and enjoy!

PER SERVING: Calories: 275 | Fat: 0.8g | Protein: 3.3g | Sodium: 7mg | Carbohydrates: 71g | Sugar: 60g

All Clear

*If your sensitive skin is prone to upsets such as rashes or reactions to cosmetics,
try this sweet and refreshing juice.*

INGREDIENTS | YIELDS 1½ CUPS

1½ cups pineapple chunks
1 large cucumber
1 apple, cored

1. Process the pineapple through an electronic juicer according to the manufacturer's directions.

2. Add the cucumber, followed by the apple.

3. Stir or shake the juice to combine the ingredients and enjoy!

PER SERVING: Calories: 199 | Fat: 0.5g | Protein: 2.2g | Sodium: 4mg | Carbohydrates: 52g | Sugar: 39g

Purple Perfection

Healthy berries help make your complexion merry and bright!

INGREDIENTS | YIELDS 1½ CUPS

1 cup Queen Anne or other sweet cherries, pitted
2 cups blueberries

1. Process the cherries through an electronic juicer according to the manufacturer's directions.

2. Add the blueberries.

3. Mix the juice to combine the ingredients and serve alone or over ice.

PER SERVING: Calories: 265 | Fat: 1g | Protein: 3.8g | Sodium: 3mg | Carbohydrates: 67g | Sugar: 49g

Blackberry Booster

Blackberries are rich in anti-inflammatory agents, which are great for conditions such as arthritis. They also help reduce puffy eyes and skin.

INGREDIENTS | YIELDS 1½ CUPS

2 cups blackberries
1 cup blueberries
½ cup raspberries

Blackberry Benefits

The high tannin content of blackberries helps tighten tissue, relieve intestinal inflammation, and reduce hemorrhoids and stomach disorders.

1. Process the blackberries through an electronic juicer according to the manufacturer's directions.

2. Add the blueberries and raspberries.

3. Stir or shake the juice to combine the ingredients and enjoy!

PER SERVING: Calories: 240 | Fat: 2.2g | Protein: 5.8g | Sodium: 5mg | Carbohydrates: 56g | Sugar: 31g

Pineapple Mango

This tropical refresher is great for the skin!

INGREDIENTS | YIELDS 2 CUPS

1 mango, peeled
1 cup pineapple chunks

How to Choose a Pineapple

Choose a pineapple that is a bit soft to the touch. The leaves should be green with no brown spots. If overripe, it will have soft spots on the skin, if underripe, it will ripen at room temperature over a few days' time.

1. Process the fruits through an electronic juicer in any order according to the manufacturer's directions.

2. Stir the juice to combine the ingredients and serve alone or over ice.

PER SERVING: Calories: 217 | Fat: 0.7g | Protein: 1.9g | Sodium: 5mg | Carbohydrates: 56g | Sugar: 46g

Tropical Treat

It's said that Christopher Columbus called papayas "the fruit of the angels."

INGREDIENTS | YIELDS 2 CUPS

1 papaya, seeded
2 small key limes or Mexican limes
1 cup unsweetened coconut milk

Papaya Facts

Papaya is an excellent source of vitamin A and vitamin C. It is a very good source of folate and potassium. In addition, it is a good source of dietary fiber, vitamin E, and vitamin K.

1. Process the papaya and limes through an electronic juicer according to the manufacturer's directions.

2. Stir in the coconut milk and serve alone or over ice.

PER SERVING: Calories: 201 | Fat: 2g | Protein: 4g | Sodium: 20mg | Carbohydrates: 53g | Sugar: 25g

Pineapple Cucumber Combo

Pineapple and cucumber are two of the best choices for juice to benefit skin, hair, and nails. If the cucumber flavor seems too strong, use an English cucumber, which has a less pronounced flavor.

INGREDIENTS | YIELDS 1 CUP

1 cup pineapple chunks
1 medium cucumber

Process the pineapple and cucumber through an electronic juicer according to the manufacturer's directions. Serve immediately.

PER SERVING: Calories: 127 | Fat: 0.5g | Protein: 3g | Sodium: 8mg | Carbohydrates: 32g | Sugar: 21g

Cherry Watermelon Combo

Sour cherries can be used in this recipe as well,
but do add a spoonful of raw honey for sweetness.

INGREDIENTS | YIELDS 1 CUP

1 cup watermelon chunks

1 cup pitted cherries

½ lime, peeled

Process the fruits in any order through an electronic juicer according to the manufacturer's directions. Serve juice immediately.

PER SERVING: Calories: 152 | Fat: 0.6g | Protein: 2.7g | Sodium: 2mg | Carbohydrates: 39g | Sugar: 29g

Life's a Bowl of Cherries?

When it comes to powerful superfoods, cherries are chock full of life-giving elements. They are loaded with antioxidants, vitamins, and compounds that help with weight loss. Nutritionists claim they can even prevent heart disease and improve mental functioning, too. The melatonin they contain plays a big role in protecting skin from the effects of the sun and helps prevent aging.

Cherry Cucumber Cooler

In addition to being terrific for encouraging longer, stronger hair and nails, cherries hold a number of benefits for the eyes, including helping to prevent cataracts and macular degeneration.

INGREDIENTS | YIELDS 1½ CUPS

1 cucumber, peeled
2 cups sweet cherries, pitted
2 celery stalks, with leaves

All about Lutein

Cherries are rich in lutein, which is known to promote cardiovascular and eye health, but it's also a powerful antioxidant. A great nonfruit source of lutein is eggs, and some researchers believe that it is best absorbed with a meal that contains some fats. So have this one for breakfast with a little extra butter on your toast!

1. Process the cucumber through your electronic juicer according to the manufacturer's directions.

2. Add the cherries.

3. Add the celery.

4. Stir or shake the juice thoroughly to combine and serve over ice.

PER SERVING: Calories: 251 | Fat: 1g | Protein: 5.7g | Sodium: 70mg | Carbohydrates: 62g | Sugar: 45g

CHAPTER 7

Fast to Fabulous

A juice fast is just what it claims to be. For a selected period of time, you'll consume only freshly made fruit and vegetable juices, along with other liquids such as water and herbal teas. There are a lot of benefits to the practice, not the least of which is cleansing and detoxing the system. Other benefits include relatively rapid weight loss, improved overall health, and increased immunity. But there are some not-so-pleasant side effects, too, and they are important to take into account before undertaking any fasting program. The first is that, depending on your level of experience with fasting, you may experience hunger, loss of energy, headaches, and a need for increased rest and relaxation. So while you needn't alter your lifestyle completely before undertaking a fast, it is important to choose a time when your schedule and the general state of your overall health allows you to derive maximum benefits. Slow down, take it easy, and allow yourself the extra bit of personal pampering you need.

How Much Is Enough?

The amount of juice you should drink per day is up to you. A 100-pound woman has different nutritional requirements than a 200-pound man. Generally speaking however, you should expect to consume between three and four quarts of juice per day during the course of your fast. A good rule of thumb is to plan to consume half fruit-based juices and half green vegetable-based juices during the course of your fast. Be particularly careful not to overdo fresh fruit juices as they can sometimes send your blood sugar levels out of balance. Most of all, listen to your body; pay attention to how you feel during a fast, and don't hesitate to ask for guidance from your doctor or health care professional before starting out.

Length of a Juice Fast

It can seem pretty intimidating to think about going without solid food for a few days, but again the choice is up to you. Juice fasting can give you great results without having to go for a long period surviving on only liquid meals, and it's not necessarily a case of the longer, the better. Experiment with mini-fasts first: Half-day fasts, one-day fasts; a combination of juices and blended or raw foods fasts can all work wonders for your health and well-being. Like any alteration to your diet, though, balance is key. Don't overdo it. Just including juicing in your daily routine along with your meals is an important start on the path to better health.

Juices for Fasting

Fast Feast

Substitute mustard greens for the turnip greens in this recipe for a peppery flavor.

INGREDIENTS | YIELDS 2 CUPS

6 medium carrots, trimmed

1 cup turnip greens

1 red bell pepper, seeded

½ cup kale

Storing Juice

If you make more juice than you can drink at once, use a vacuum seal device and store the juice in the refrigerator. Most juices will retain their nutrients for at least twenty-four hours when sealed and refrigerated, the exception being the more volatile, citrus-based juices, which should be consumed as soon as possible.

1. Process the carrots through an electronic juicer according to the manufacturer's directions.

2. Add the turnip greens, followed by the pepper.

3. Add the kale.

4. Stir or shake the juice to combine the ingredients and enjoy!

PER SERVING: Calories: 255 | Fat: 2g | Protein: 7.7g | Sodium: 359mg | Carbohydrates: 56g | Sugar: 25g

Luscious Liquid Lunch

Gorgeous color and lively flavor! If cilantro is not to your liking, substitute fresh parsley, or a combination of parsley and mint.

INGREDIENTS | YIELDS 1½ CUPS

2 kale leaves

½ cup spinach

½ cup cilantro

2 apples, cored

1 pear, cored

½ lemon, peeled

1 (1-inch) piece fresh ginger

1. Process the kale, spinach, and cilantro through an electronic juicer according to the manufacturer's directions.

2. Add the apples, followed by the pear.

3. Add the lemon and the ginger.

4. Stir or shake the juice to combine the ingredients and enjoy!

PER SERVING: Calories: 311 | Fat: 1.5g | Protein: 4.7g | Sodium: 43mg | Carbohydrates: 79g | Sugar: 49g

Powerhouse

This juice provides powerful nutrition in a glass.

INGREDIENTS | YIELDS 1½ CUPS

4 celery stalks, with leaves

1 bunch parsley

2 cups spinach

⅓ medium cucumber

2 carrots, trimmed

1 beet, trimmed and tailed

2 leaves Swiss chard

Give It a Squeeze

Some people find the flavor of greens-based juices less than appetizing, but adding a healthy squeeze of lemon juice or a dash of hot sauce can do a lot to perk up the flavor and tickle your taste buds.

1. Process the celery and parsley through an electronic juicer according to the manufacturer's directions.

2. Add the spinach, followed by the cucumber and the carrots.

3. Add the beet and the Swiss chard.

4. Mix the juice thoroughly to combine the ingredients and serve alone or over ice.

PER SERVING: Calories: 170 | Fat: 1.6g | Protein: 9.2g | Sodium: 548mg | Carbohydrates: 35g | Sugar: 16g

Watermelon Fast

Some juicers swear by the effectiveness of single-ingredient, one-day fasts for cleansing the system, losing weight, and restoring the body's alkaline balance. Many favor watermelon for its ability to hydrate and keep you feeling full while at the same time flushing away toxins.

INGREDIENTS | YIELDS 6¾ CUPS (3 SERVINGS)

5–6-pound watermelon, divided into thirds

Juice only one third of the watermelon for breakfast, lunch, and dinner. Consume each portion immediately after juicing.

PER SERVING: Calories: 224 | Fat: 1g | Protein: 4.5g | Sodium: 7.5mg | Carbohydrates: 56g | Sugar: 46g

Blues Buster

Fasting can bring on some mood swings, so if you feel your good humor slipping away, try this.

INGREDIENTS | YIELDS 1 CUP

1 cup broccoli florets
½ cup spinach leaves
4 leaves Swiss chard
½ red bell pepper, seeded

1. Process the broccoli through an electronic juicer according to the manufacturer's directions.

2. Add the spinach, followed by the chard.

3. Add the bell pepper.

4. Mix the juice thoroughly to combine the ingredients and serve alone or over ice.

PER SERVING: Calories: 89 | Fat: 1g | Protein: 7g | Sodium: 339mg | Carbohydrates: 17g | Sugar: 6g

Carrot Mango Cup

This is a great combination of flavors that is both tasty and filling.

INGREDIENTS | YIELDS 1 CUP

3 large carrots, trimmed
1 mango, peeled and seeded

1. Process the carrots and mango through an electronic juicer according to the manufacturer's directions.

2. Serve the juice alone or over ice.

PER SERVING: Calories: 223 | Fat: 1g | Protein: 3g | Sodium: 153mg | Carbohydrates: 55g | Sugar: 40g

Apricot Cooler

This makes a perfect choice when you're craving something sweet.

INGREDIENTS | YIELDS 1 CUP

4 fresh apricots, pitted
1 slice honeydew melon
1 pear, cored
½ cup raspberries

1. Process the apricots and melon through an electronic juicer according to the manufacturer's directions.

2. Add the pear, followed by the raspberries.

3. Mix the juice to combine the ingredients and serve over ice.

PER SERVING: Calories: 246 | Fat: 1.3g | Protein: 4g | Sodium: 34mg | Carbohydrates: 61g | Sugar: 43g

Sunset Supper

This juice has great color and a fantastic flavor perfect for any time of the day!
For easier juicing, cut the greens from the beets and add them separately.

INGREDIENTS | YIELDS 1½ CUPS

5 carrots, trimmed
2 cucumbers
2 medium sugar beets, complete with greens

1. Process the carrots through an electronic juicer according to the manufacturer's directions.

2. Add the cucumbers, one at a time.

3. Add the beets, followed by the greens.

4. Mix the juice to combine the ingredients and serve over ice.

PER SERVING: Calories: 308 | Fat: 1.8g | Protein: 10g | Sodium: 388mg | Carbohydrates: 72g | Sugar: 38g

Orange Spinach Delight

Definitely a delightful combo, the greens take a back seat
to the lively fresh taste of the orange in this recipe.

INGREDIENTS | YIELDS 1½ CUPS

4 oranges, peeled
2 cups fresh spinach
1 cup parsley

Ask an Athlete

Many professional athletes praise the power of parsley to boost performance. So if your juice fast has left you feeling a little low on energy, be sure to throw in a handful to your fasting favorites.

1. Process the oranges through an electronic juicer according to the manufacturer's directions.

2. Add the spinach and parsley.

3. Mix the juice to combine the ingredients and serve over ice.

PER SERVING: Calories: 215 | Fat: 1g | Protein: 7g | Sodium: 81mg | Carbohydrates: 51g | Sugar: 36g

Collard Classic

Red pepper and tomato provide a nice flavor balance for the greens in this recipe.

INGREDIENTS | YIELDS 1½ CUPS

1 kale leaf
1 collard leaf
1 celery stalk, with leaves
1 carrot, trimmed
½ red pepper, seeded
1 large tomato
½ cup arugula
¼ cup parsley

Collard Greens

A staple of traditional Southern cooking, collards are rich in nutrition. They contain protein, thiamin, niacin, and potassium, as well as vitamin A, vitamin C, vitamin E, vitamin K, riboflavin, vitamin B$_6$, folate, calcium, and manganese. It doesn't get much healthier than that!

1. Process the kale and collard leaves through an electronic juicer according to the manufacturer's directions.

2. Add the celery, followed by the carrot and the red pepper.

3. Add the tomato, the arugula, and the parsley.

4. Mix the juice to combine the ingredients and serve over ice.

PER SERVING: Calories: 94 | Fat: 1.5g | Protein: 4.5g | Sodium: 102mg | Carbohydrates: 19g | Sugar: 8.5g

Cantaloupe Cinnamon Cooler

On a juice fast, you can treat yourself to a whole melon without guilt!
Plus, melons contain lots of soluble fiber, which helps fill you up and satisfies those hunger pangs.

INGREDIENTS | YIELDS 2 CUPS

1 whole cantaloupe
½ teaspoon cinnamon

1. Peel and seed the melon, then cut it into chunks.

2. Process the melon chunks through an electronic juicer according to the manufacturer's directions.

3. Add the cinnamon and mix. Serve the juice alone or over ice.

PER SERVING: Calories: 190 | Fat: 1g | Protein: 4.6g | Sodium: 88mg | Carbohydrates: 45g | Sugar: 43g

Ginger Celery Cooler

Distinctly Asian flavor makes this perfect for a summer snack! Add a dash of soy sauce for added zip.

INGREDIENTS | YIELDS 1 CUP

3 stalks celery, with leaves
1 small clove of fresh garlic, peeled
1 (1-inch) piece fresh ginger
1 cucumber
2 scallions, trimmed

1. Process the celery through an electronic juicer according to the manufacturer's directions.

2. Add the garlic and the ginger, followed by the cucumber and the scallions.

3. Mix the juice to combine the ingredients and serve.

PER SERVING: Calories: 94 | Fat: 1g | Protein: 3.7g | Sodium: 107mg | Carbohydrates: 20g | Sugar: 8g

Satsuma Fennel Treat

Satsuma, or honey citrus, are small mandarin oranges that become widely available from October through Christmas.

INGREDIENTS | YIELDS 1 CUP

3 satsuma, peeled
½ fennel bulb
¼ lemon or lime, peeled

How to Choose the Best Satsuma

Choose fruit that is small but heavy for its size for the greatest juice yield. Satsuma is prone to mold, so store in the refrigerator.

1. Process the satsuma segments through an electronic juicer according to the manufacturer's directions.

2. Add the fennel bulb, followed by the lemon or lime.

3. Mix the juice thoroughly to combine the ingredients and serve alone or over ice.

PER SERVING: Calories: 161 | Fat: 1g | Protein: 3.5g | Sodium: 65mg | Carbohydrates: 40g | Sugar: 24g

Red Velvet

This vibrantly colored juice is not exactly a piece of cake, but sweet and satisfying all the same!

INGREDIENTS | YIELDS 1½ CUPS

3 carrots, trimmed
2 large Granny Smith apples, cored
1 orange, peeled
¼ sugar beet, tailed and trimmed

Sugar in the Morning

When fasting, it's best to consume sweet fruit juices in the morning, go to green juices at lunch, and confine yourself to simple, one- or two-fruit combinations in the late afternoon for a quick pick-me-up.

1. Process the carrots and apples through an electronic juicer according to the manufacturer's directions.

2. Add the orange segments, followed by the beet.

3. Mix the juice thoroughly to combine the ingredients and serve alone or over ice.

PER SERVING: Calories: 245 | Fat: 1g | Protein: 3g | Sodium: 121mg | Carbohydrates: 62g | Sugar: 43g

Vitamin Mixer

Alfalfa sprouts are low in calories but high in protein, with a fabulous mix of vitamins to boot.

1 lemon, peeled
2 cups alfalfa sprouts
1 (1-inch) piece fresh ginger
2 carrots, trimmed
3 cucumbers
½ cup parsley

1. Process the lemon through an electronic juicer according to the manufacturer's directions.

2. Add the sprouts, followed by the ginger and the carrots.

3. Add the cucumbers one at a time, followed by the parsley.

4. Mix the juice thoroughly to combine the ingredients and serve alone or over ice.

PER SERVING: Calories: 237 | Fat: 2.4g | Protein: 11g | Sodium: 110mg | Carbohydrates: 54g | Sugar: 21g

Gadzooks

As this recipe proves, sometimes the simplest combinations provide maximum benefits.

INGREDIENTS | YIELDS 1 CUP

3 or 4 medium zucchini
2 stalks celery, with leaves

Zucchini Benefits

If you grow a garden, juicing is a wonderful way to rid yourself of too many zucchini. Very low in calories, zucchini is rich in vitamin A and potassium, a heart-friendly electrolyte that helps reduce blood pressure and heart rates by countering the effects of sodium.

1. Process the squash and the celery through an electronic juicer according to the manufacturer's directions.

2. Mix or shake the juice to combine the ingredients and serve alone or over ice.

PER SERVING: Calories: 112 | Fat: 2g | Protein: 7.6g | Sodium: 111mg | Carbohydrates: 20g | Sugar: 16g

Nutrition Star

The starfruit, also known as carambola, is cultivated throughout the tropics. It provides vitamins C and A, as well as iron and dietary fiber.

INGREDIENTS | YIELDS 1 CUP

3 starfruit
1 slice honeydew melon

1. Process the starfruit and melon through an electronic juicer according to the manufacturer's directions.

2. Mix or shake the juice to combine the ingredients and serve alone or over ice.

PER SERVING: Calories: 145 | Fat: 1g | Protein: 3.5g | Sodium: 36mg | Carbohydrates: 33g | Sugar: 24g

Cauliflower Combo

Another feast for your fast, this is the juicing equivalent of a big chef's salad!

Cauliflower Caution

Like other members of the cruciferous family, excessive consumption of cauliflower may cause swelling of the thyroid gland and thyroid hormone deficiency. This is due to the presence of certain plant compounds known as goitrogens. So if you have a history of thyroid dysfunction, limit your cruciferous intake.

1. Process the cauliflower through an electronic juicer according to the manufacturer's directions.

2. Add the cabbage, followed by the pepper and the scallions.

3. Add the lettuce and the tomatoes.

4. Whisk or shake the juice thoroughly to combine the ingredients and serve alone or over ice.

PER SERVING: Calories: 159 | Fat: 2g | Protein: 9.4g | Sodium: 85mg | Carbohydrates: 33g | Sugar: 17g

Eden Elixir

Some say Eve ate an apple, others say a pomegranate. Either way, this will put you in paradise.

INGREDIENTS | YIELDS 1½ CUPS

6 carrots, trimmed

2 kale leaves

4 Brussels sprouts

1 apple, cored or ¼ cup pomegranate seeds

Brussels Sprouts and Cancer Prevention

Three major systems in the body that figure into cancer risk are the body's detox system, its antioxidant system, and its anti-inflammatory system. Chronic imbalances in any of these three systems can increase risk of cancer, and when imbalances in all three systems occur simultaneously, the risk of cancer increases. The good news is that Brussels sprouts have been seen to have a significant impact of the health of each of these systems without the negative impact on the thyroids sometimes associated with the cruciferous group.

1. Process the carrots through an electronic juicer according to the manufacturer's directions.

2. Add the kale, followed by the Brussels sprouts and the apple or pomegranate.

3. Whisk the juice to combine the ingredients and serve alone or over ice.

PER SERVING: Calories: 236 | Fat: 1.4g | Protein: 7.5g | Sodium: 250mg | Carbohydrates: 55g | Sugar: 27g

CHAPTER 8

Veggie-Only Juices

Among juice enthusiasts, there's a mixed school of thought as to whether you should combine fruits and vegetables in your juicing practice. Purists insist that the greatest nutritional benefits are derived when the body is given similar foods in juice form—exclusively greens for example, when you need the chlorophyll boost, or exclusively red or orange veggies when you want the carotene benefits. Others insist that adding fruits to your veggie juice will affect your blood sugar, and some choose to avoid the sugar and carbohydrates of fruit juices altogether. And too, there are those who just don't enjoy a complex mix of flavors. Some kids won't go near the green stuff if it touches their potatoes on the plate, while others gleefully mix their peas and mashed potatoes before they'll eat either one!

Juice According to Your Preference

In truth, there's very little in the way of nutritional data to support the idea that juiced nutrition is better absorbed one way or another, so once again, it's all a matter of a) dietary balance and b) personal preference. If you find that you derive more benefit from exclusively vegetable juices, by all means, skip the sugars. But if you turn up your nose at a juice made from leafy greens, and just can't get it down without some sweetening, then by all means add the apple. In any event, don't be afraid to experiment; listen to your body and let it be your guide. After all, you won't derive the benefits of any juice if you don't try it!

Very Veggie Juices

Celery Asparagus Tonic

Two superfoods combine in one great juice that tastes like springtime!

INGREDIENTS | YIELDS 1½ CUPS

5 stalks celery, with leaves

10–12 asparagus stalks, woody ends removed

¼ cup mint leaves

1. Process the celery through an electronic juicer according to the manufacturer's directions

2. Add the asparagus, followed by the mint.

3. Mix the juice to combine the ingredients and serve alone or over ice.

PER SERVING: Calories: 86 | Fat: 1g | Protein: 6.3g | Sodium: 185mg | Carbohydrates: 16g | Sugar: 7g

The French Connection

Fresh haricot vert, or green beans, are juiced and flavored with fresh tarragon in this elegant concoction.

INGREDIENTS | YIELDS 1 CUP

½ pound haricot vert

1 large cucumber

¼ cup fresh tarragon

3 scallions, trimmed

1. Process the beans through an electronic juicer according to the manufacturer's directions.

2. Add the cucumber, followed by the tarragon and the scallions.

3. Whisk or shake the juice to combine the ingredients and serve over ice.

PER SERVING: Calories: 91 | Fat: 0.7g | Protein: 5g | Sodium: 20mg | Carbohydrates: 20g | Sugar: 10g

Bring on the Beans!

In addition to the protein green beans provide, the antioxidant capacity of green beans has been shown to be greater than similar foods in the pea and bean families, for example, snow peas or winged beans.

Cabbage and Carrot Combo

You may also substitute red cabbage in this recipe, but be aware that while red cabbage is slightly higher in nutrients than the white or green varieties, it does have a stronger flavor.

INGREDIENTS | YIELDS 1 CUP

8 ounces white or green cabbage, chopped

3 large carrots, trimmed

Read the Directions . . .
Cabbage, because of its high fiber content, can be challenging to some juicers, so be sure to check the manufacturer's guidelines.

1. Process the cabbage and carrots through an electronic juicer according to the manufacturer's directions.

2. Whisk or shake the juice to combine the ingredients and serve over ice.

PER SERVING: Calories: 144 | Fat: 0.7g | Protein: 4.8g | Sodium: 189mg | Carbohydrates: 33g | Sugar: 17g

Watercress Cocktail

Watercress adds a peppery punch to the taste of this juice along with some powerful nutrients.

INGREDIENTS | YIELDS 1 CUP

4 ounces watercress

3 large carrots, trimmed

2 stalks celery, with leaves

1. Process the watercress and carrots through an electronic juicer according to the manufacturer's directions.

2. Add the celery.

3. Whisk or shake the juice to combine the ingredients and serve over ice.

PER SERVING: Calories: 113 | Fat: 0.8g | Protein: 5g | Sodium: 258mg | Carbohydrates: 24g | Sugar: 12g

Hale and Hearty

This savory green juice is also great with a dash of lemon juice or hot sauce.

INGREDIENTS | YIELDS 1½ CUPS

½ cup romaine lettuce, chopped
½ cup green beans
¾ cup Brussels sprouts
½ cup chopped Jerusalem artichokes
2 large carrots, trimmed

Jerusalem Artichokes

Jerusalem artichokes are actually the tubers of a tall flowering plant. They have a taste and texture much like that of water chestnuts.

1. Process the lettuce and green beans through an electronic juicer according to the manufacturer's directions.

2. Add the Brussels sprouts and Jerusalem artichokes, followed by the carrots.

3. Whisk or shake the juice to combine the ingredients and serve over ice.

PER SERVING: Calories: 163 | Fat: 0.7g | Protein: 6.3g | Sodium: 124mg | Carbohydrates: 37g | Sugar: 17g

Beet Bliss

Adding onion and garlic to this root veggie combo results in great flavor and extra nutrients, too!

INGREDIENTS | YIELDS 1 CUP

2 large carrots, trimmed
1 medium beet, trimmed and tailed
½ cup watercress
¼ cup red onion, peeled and chopped
1 clove garlic, peeled

For the Love of Garlic

Sautéed, fresh, or roasted, garlic is an excellent source of minerals, vitamins, and enzymes essential to good health. The bulbs are one of the richest sources of potassium, iron, calcium, magnesium, manganese, zinc, and selenium.

1. Process the carrots, beet, and watercress through an electronic juicer according to the manufacturer's directions.

2. Add the onion and the garlic.

3. Whisk or shake the juice to combine the ingredients and serve over ice.

PER SERVING: Calories: 116 | Fat: 0.5g | Protein: 3.6g | Sodium: 172mg | Carbohydrates: 26g | Sugar: 14g

Golden Glow

*Yellow tomatoes, yellow summer squash, and yellow wax beans
combine for a beautiful color and a mild, pleasing flavor.*

INGREDIENTS | YIELDS 1 CUP

4 yellow pear tomatoes
1 yellow summer squash
1 cup fresh yellow wax beans

Let the Sunshine In

Yellow fruits and vegetables are teeming with carotenoids and bioflavonoids, which are a class of plant pigments that function as antioxidants. Sunny-colored foods also have an abundance of vitamin C. These nutrients will help your heart, vision, digestion, and immune systems. Other benefits of naturally yellow foods include maintenance of healthy skin, wound healing, and stronger bones and teeth.

1. Process the tomatoes through an electronic juicer according to the manufacturer's directions.

2. Add the squash, followed by the beans.

3. Stir the juice to combine the ingredients and serve alone or over ice.

PER SERVING: Calories: 232 | Fat: 1g | Protein: 14g | Sodium: 59mg | Carbohydrates: 44g | Sugar: 8.5g

The Iron Maiden

This juice is named the Iron Maiden because of its rich supply of the mineral.

INGREDIENTS | YIELDS 2 CUPS

4 carrots, trimmed
½ cup chopped spinach
4 romaine lettuce leaves
½ turnip, including greens
¼ cup chopped fresh parsley

1. Process the carrots through an electronic juicer according to the manufacturer's directions.

2. Add the spinach, followed by the lettuce.

3. Add the turnip and greens, followed by the parsley.

4. Whisk or shake the juice to combine the ingredients and serve over ice.

PER SERVING: Calories: 179 | Fat: 1.2g | Protein: 6g | Sodium: 320mg | Carbohydrates: 40g | Sugar: 20g

Cucumber Pepper Potion

Sweet bell peppers are an excellent source of vitamins A and C. Choose cucumbers with firm skin and no shriveling or soft spots.

INGREDIENTS | YIELDS 1 CUP

1 cucumber, peeled
1 celery stalk, with leaves
½ green bell pepper, seeded

1. Process the cucumber through an electronic juicer according to the manufacturer's directions.

2. Add the celery, followed by the bell pepper.

3. Stir the juice to combine the ingredients and serve over ice.

PER SERVING: Calories: 63 | Fat: 0.5g | Protein: 2.7g | Sodium: 39mg | Carbohydrates: 15g | Sugar: 7g

Cucumbers

Cucumbers are available year round. Store them unwashed in your refrigerator for up to ten days. Wash them just before using. Leftover cucumbers can be refrigerated again; just tightly wrap them in plastic and they will keep for up to five days.

Good Old Gazpacho Juice

Here is the pure juice form of the traditional cold soup.

INGREDIENTS | YIELDS 2 CUPS

2 large tomatoes
½ green pepper, seeded
½ red pepper, seeded
1 fresh jalapeño pepper, seeded
4 scallions, trimmed
1 clove garlic, peeled

Heat in Jalapeños
Most of the fiery heat of fresh jalapeños is avoided if you carefully remove the seeds and ribs of the pepper before juicing.

1. Process the tomatoes through an electronic juicer according to the manufacturer's directions.

2. Add the peppers, followed by the scallions and the garlic.

3. Whisk or shake the juice to combine the ingredients and serve over ice.

PER SERVING: Calories: 107 | Fat: 1.6g | Protein: 4.8g | Sodium: 28mg | Carbohydrates: 23g | Sugar: 14g

Liquid Pickle

Cucumbers are almost all water, yet hold a wealth of restorative powers. This recipe is wonderful for a hot summer's day, because this dill-flavored juice contains none of the salt of regular pickles.

INGREDIENTS | YIELDS 1½ CUPS

2 medium cucumbers
½ cup fresh dill
4 scallions, trimmed
½ cup chopped Swiss chard

Cucumber Benefits
Cucumber has high alkaline levels, and helps to regulate the body's blood pH to neutralize acidity. It also helps with overall hydration and regulates blood pressure. The hard skin of the cucumber is rich in fiber and a range of minerals that include magnesium, molybdenum, silica, and potassium.

1. Process the cucumbers through an electronic juicer according to the manufacturer's directions.

2. Add the dill, followed by the scallions and the Swiss chard.

3. Whisk or shake the juice to combine the ingredients and serve over ice.

PER SERVING: Calories: 108 | Fat: 0.9g | Protein: 4.8g | Sodium: 60mg | Carbohydrates: 25g | Sugar: 12g

Dandelion Delight

So called "wild" foods such as dandelions and the nettle greens included in this recipe are not just inexpensive to the point of being free, depending on where you live, but really can serve as a reminder of just how bountiful Nature can be.

INGREDIENTS | YIELDS 2 CUPS

1 cup chopped dandelion greens

1 cup chopped nettle greens

1 cucumber

How to Pick Nettle Greens

If nettles aren't available at your local farmers' market, choose young plants and take only the top 4 or 5 inches from each plant. Wear gloves and long pants to avoid getting "stung." As for nutrition? A lot like spinach, but better. High in iron, calcium, vitamin C, and a slew of other nutrients, nettles have been used fresh and dried for nutritional and medical uses over the years.

1. Wash the greens thoroughly before chopping. Process the greens through an electronic juicer according to the manufacturer's directions.

2. Add the cucumber.

3. Whisk the juice thoroughly to combine the ingredients and serve over ice.

PER SERVING: Calories: 78 | Fat: 0.5g | Protein: 5g | Sodium: 34mg | Carbohydrates: 17g | Sugar: 7g

Dandelion Dandy

Got dandelions? Juice them! Dandelion greens rank in the top four green vegetables in overall nutritional value. This recipe bends the veggies-only rule for this chapter with the addition of lemon juice, but if you prefer, substitute a tomato instead.

INGREDIENTS | YIELDS 2 CUPS

1 pound carrots, trimmed

1 lemon, peeled

¾ cup dandelion greens, chopped

Dandelions

Dandelions are also nature's richest green vegetable source of beta-carotene, from which vitamin A is created, as well as being particularly rich in fiber, potassium, iron, calcium, magnesium, phosphorus, and the B vitamins, thiamine, and riboflavin, and are a good source of protein.

1. Process the carrots, lemon, and dandelion greens through an electronic juicer according to the manufacturer's directions.

2. Whisk or shake the juice to combine the ingredients and serve over ice.

PER SERVING: Calories: 211 | Fat: 1.3g | Protein: 6g | Sodium: 320mg | Carbohydrates: 50g | Sugar: 23g

Celery Chervil Cocktail

The mild mannered celery gets a whole new character with the addition of fresh chervil.

Chervil

Related to and with many of the same nutritional properties as parsley, chervil has a faint flavor of licorice.

1. Process the celery though an electronic juicer according to the manufacturer's directions.

2. Add the chervil.

3. Serve the juice alone or over ice.

   PER SERVING: Calories: 48 | Fat: 0.5g | Protein: 2g | Sodium: 192mg | Carbohydrates: 9g | Sugar: 5g

Bean Sprout Bliss

Simplicity itself, this light and lovely combination has powerful nutritional benefits.

INGREDIENTS | YIELDS 1 CUP

1 cup bean sprouts
2 stalks celery, with leaves
1 medium cucumber

Why Sprouts Are So Healthy

As a seed sprouts, it activates many different metabolic systems. It converts some of its sugar content into vitamin C, to act as an antioxidant above the soil. It also begins to synthesize a variety of new enzymes, many of them necessary to handle oxygen metabolism.

1. Process the bean sprouts and celery through an electronic juicer according to the manufacturer's directions.

2. Add the cucumber.

3. Mix the juice to combine the ingredients and serve over ice.

PER SERVING: Calories: 111 | Fat: 1.3g | Protein: 10g | Sodium: 81mg | Carbohydrates: 20g | Sugar: 6.5g

Carrot Cabbage Cleanse

Another recipe to prove that sometimes simplicity is everything! Both carrots and cabbage are not only rich in nutrients but have great cleansing effects on the system.

INGREDIENTS | YIELDS 1½ CUPS

5 carrots, trimmed
¼ red cabbage, roughly chopped

1. Process the carrots and the cabbage through an electronic juicer according to the manufacturer's directions.

2. Mix the juice to combine the ingredients and serve alone or over ice.

PER SERVING: Calories: 204 | Fat: 1g | Protein: 6g | Sodium: 289mg | Carbohydrates: 47g | Sugar: 24g

The Radical Radish

Radishes are rich in folic acid, vitamin C, and anthocyanins. These nutrients make it a very effective cancer-fighting food. It is said that radish is effective in fighting oral cancer, colon cancer, and intestinal cancer as well as kidney and stomach cancers.

INGREDIENTS | YIELDS 1 CUP

1 cup radishes, trimmed and tailed
½ cup parsley
1 medium zucchini

1. Process the radishes through an electronic juicer according to the manufacturer's directions.

2. Add the parsley, followed by the zucchini.

3. Mix or shake the juice to combine the ingredients and serve alone or over ice.

PER SERVING: Calories: 62 | Fat: 1g | Protein: 4g | Sodium: 77mg | Carbohydrates: 12g | Sugar: 7g

Popeye's Secret Blend

This juice is high in magnesium, which is a natural muscle relaxant. Spinach is very rich in iron and a great source of vitamins A and C. The leaves tend to be gritty, so rinse them thoroughly.

INGREDIENTS | YIELDS 1 CUP

1 cup spinach leaves
1 cucumber, peeled
2 carrots, trimmed and peeled

1. Process the spinach through an electronic juicer according to the manufacturer's directions.

2. Add the cucumber, followed by the carrots.

3. Mix or shake the juice to combine the ingredients and serve alone or over ice.

PER SERVING: Calories: 111 | Fat: 0.7g | Protein: 4g | Sodium: 129mg | Carbohydrates: 25g | Sugar: 12g

Kohlrabi Cure-All

Kohlrabi is a root vegetable that tastes like a cross between turnips, radishes, and cabbage. For that reason, it's best to combine it with other milder veggies or water to dilute the strong flavor a bit.

INGREDIENTS | YIELDS 1 CUP

1 small kohlrabi, cut into quarters, with greens
1 medium cucumber
1 medium zucchini
1 clove garlic, peeled

Kolhrabi Facts

Cultivated since Roman times, kohlrabi can be found in a purple globe variety or a lighter apple green. Kohlrabi leaves or tops, like the bulbs, are very nutritious, abundant in carotenes, vitamin A, vitamin K, minerals, and B-complex group of vitamins.

1. Process the kohlrabi and its greens through an electronic juicer according to the manufacturer's directions.

2. Add the cucumber, followed by the zucchini and the garlic.

3. Shake the juice to combine the ingredients, dilute with water to taste, or serve over ice.

PER SERVING: Calories: 117 | Fat: 1g | Protein: 5.6g | Sodium: 103mg | Carbohydrates: 25g | Sugar: 14g

Chayote Juice

There are myriad claims among chayote fans about its fantastic abilities to lower blood pressure and regulate blood sugar levels in those who suffer from diabetes.

INGREDIENTS | YIELDS 1½ CUPS

1 medium chayote squash, peeled and pitted
1 cucumber
1 carrot, trimmed

Chayote Squash

Chayote squash belongs to the summer squash family and is considered, along with corn and beans, by indigenous peoples of Mexico and the Southwest to be one of the "three sisters," the staples of their diet for centuries.

1. Process the chayote through an electronic juicer according to the manufacturer's directions.

2. Add the cucumber, followed by the carrot.

3. Mix the juice to combine the ingredients and serve over ice.

PER SERVING: Calories: 113 | Fat: 0.7g | Protein: 4.2g | Sodium: 59mg | Carbohydrates: 26g | Sugar: 11g

Pumpkin Juice

Though generally thought of as a fruit, pumpkin is actually a squash, belonging to the same family as other summer squashes. Use a heavier duty juicer for this one, especially if you're tackling a bigger pumpkin!

INGREDIENTS | YIELDS 1 CUP

2 cups chopped pumpkin
½ cup water
1 (1-inch) piece fresh ginger
3 tablespoons raw honey

Don't Toss That Pumpkin!

Once your pumpkin has done its Halloween duty, slice it into segments and freeze. The squash can be repurposed for all kinds of uses. When juicing pumpkin, reserve the pulp and freeze to use in pies, baking, or other recipes. Just be sure to use or freeze your pumpkin within 24 hours.

1. Process the pumpkin through an electronic juicer according to the manufacturer's directions.

2. Add the water, ginger, and honey.

3. Mix or shake the juice to combine the ingredients and serve alone or over ice.

PER SERVING: Calories: 272 | Fat: 0.5g | Protein: 3g | Sodium: 10mg | Carbohydrates: 71g | Sugar: 55g

CHAPTER 9

Fun Fruit

Fruit juicing has gotten something of a bad rap in certain quarters. Because fruit juice contains sugar, there are those who automatically dismiss its many health benefits. But it's important to remember that the sugars contained in fruit juices are natural sugars, unrefined, and essentially healthy. While there are those who caution against fruit juicing and what may happen to your blood sugar and insulin levels, especially during a juice fast, the majority of healthy people can absorb the naturally occurring sugars in fruit juice just fine. Along with the natural sugars found in 100 percent fruit juice, you also get a nutrient dense, disease-fighting treat that is naturally low in fat and sodium. So, once again, balance is key. Sugar, even if it's naturally occurring sugar, still means calories. If you go overboard with juice, you may be consuming too many calories, so it only makes good sense to alternate fruit and vegetable juices in your juicing practice.

Choose Fruits Wisely

While just about any fruit can be successfully juiced, never overlook the obvious popular choices. Chances are, if it's readily available from a juice manufacturer, it will be even better if you juice it fresh yourself. Oranges, for example, are one of the best possible choices. Orange juice is higher in vitamin C than other juices, very high in potassium, a good source of folate, and it contains antioxidants. Apples come in a close second, followed by tomatoes, pineapples, grapefruit, apricots, grapes, blueberries, black cherries, and cranberries.

Just remember, fruit juice really is good for you, you just have to make the right selections. Adding 100 percent pure fruit juice to your diet is a great way to meet the recommended daily 5–9 servings of fruits and vegetables, as long as you enjoy it in moderation.

Fabulous Fruit Juices

OJ Tango

*Orange juice is packed full of vitamins and antioxidants,
but it's given an extra kick of nutrition when it's paired with tangerines.*

INGREDIENTS | YIELDS 1½ CUPS

3 large Valencia oranges, peeled
3 tangerines, peeled

1. Process the fruit in any order through an electronic juice processor according to the manufacturer's directions.

2. Serve immediately.

PER SERVING: Calories: 308 | Fat: 1.3g | Protein: 5.3g | Sodium: 7mg | Carbohydrates: 77g | Sugar: 61g

Twin Citrus

One story of the clementine's origin is that it was an accidental hybrid said to have been discovered by Father Clément Rodier in the garden of his orphanage in Algeria around 1900, but there is evidence that these fruits were grown in China centuries earlier.

INGREDIENTS | YIELDS 1½ CUPS

3 large Valencia oranges, peeled
4 or 5 clementines, peeled

What's the Difference?

Tangerines tend to be tarter than clementines and have seeds, while clementines do not. The smaller clementines also have less acid and so might be the better choice for those who are sensitive to the acids in citrus fruits.

1. Process the fruit in any order through an electronic juice processor according to the manufacturer's directions.

2. Serve immediately.

PER SERVING: Calories: 338 | Fat: 2g | Protein: 6.2g | Sodium: 6mg | Carbohydrates: 83g | Sugar: 32g

Blueberry Citrus Juice

The sweetness of the berries provides a wonderful counterpoint to the tartness of citrus.

INGREDIENTS | YIELDS 1½ CUPS

2 cups blueberries

1 large ruby red or pink grapefruit, peeled

1. Process the fruits in any order through an electronic juicer according to the manufacturer's directions.

2. Serve immediately.

PER SERVING: Calories: 274 | Fat: 1.3g | Protein: 4.2g | Sodium: 3mg | Carbohydrates: 69g | Sugar: 52g

Citrus Surprise

The surprise is that citrus pairs amazingly well with the bit of ginger in this recipe. It's best to peel larger limes, but when using smaller, thin-skinned Mexican limes, peeling isn't necessary.

INGREDIENTS | YIELDS 1½ CUPS

1 pink grapefruit, peeled

2 large oranges, peeled

2 medium limes, or 6 Mexican limes

1 (½-inch) piece fresh ginger

1. Process the grapefruit through an electronic juicer according to the manufacturer's directions.

2. Add the orange segments, followed by the limes and the ginger.

3. Serve immediately over ice if desired.

PER SERVING: Calories: 313 | Fat: 1.2g | Protein: 6.5g | Sodium: 4.4mg | Carbohydrates: 81g | Sugar: 54g

Mexican Limes

There's a lot of overlap in the world of limes. Mexican limes are, like key limes, smaller and somewhat tarter in flavor than regular limes. Traditional key limes were grown in Florida but are now also grown in Mexico! If you're using larger limes for this recipe, do peel them to avoid adding any bitterness to the flavor. Smaller limes have thin peels and little of the bitter pith, so it's not necessary.

Grapple Juice

Grapefruit, apple, and pineapple combine with watermelon for scrumptious results!

INGREDIENTS | YIELDS 2 CUPS

1 large grapefruit, peeled
1 apple, cored
2 cups fresh pineapple chunks
1 large slice watermelon, or 1½ cups watermelon chunks

Juice Yields

Yields for fresh juices can vary by as much as 4–5 ounces, depending on the efficiency of your juicer.

1. Process the grapefruit through an electronic juicer according to the manufacturer's directions.

2. Add the apple, followed by the pineapple and the watermelon.

3. Mix or shake ingredients to blend and serve over ice.

PER SERVING: Calories: 409 | Fat: 1.3g | Protein: 6g | Sodium: 6mg | Carbohydrates: 105g | Sugar: 84g

Orange Ginger Ale

Add sparkling water or seltzer to this one for that bubbly, festive feeling!

INGREDIENTS | YIELDS 1½ CUPS

3 oranges, peeled
1 (1-inch) piece fresh ginger, or to taste
¾ cup seltzer or sparkling water

1. Process the oranges and the ginger through an electronic juicer according to the manufacturer's directions.

2. Add the seltzer or sparkling water and serve over ice.

PER SERVING: Calories: 186 | Fat: 0.4g | Protein: 3.7g | Sodium: 0.2mg | Carbohydrates: 46g | Sugar: 36g

Tropical Sunrise

Beautiful color and fabulous flavor will have you dreaming of the islands . . .

INGREDIENTS | YIELDS 2 CUPS

2 oranges, peeled

1 ruby red grapefruit, peeled

¾ cup pineapple chunks

¾ cup strawberries

Strawberry Facts

In a recent study, researchers ranked strawberries third among all U.S. foods including spices, seasonings, fruits, and vegetables for their antioxidant qualities.

1. Process the oranges and the grapefruit through an electronic juicer according to the manufacturer's directions.

2. Add the pineapple, followed by the strawberries.

3. Whisk or shake the juice to combine the ingredients and serve alone or over ice.

PER SERVING: Calories: 250 | Fat: 1g | Protein: 4.5g | Sodium: 2mg | Carbohydrates: 63g | Sugar: 49g

Watermelon Pear Cocktail

Beautifully refreshing, this juice is the perfect choice for a lazy summer afternoon. For added nutrition, you could throw in a handful of blackberries.

INGREDIENTS | YIELDS 2½ CUPS (2 SERVINGS)

2 Anjou or Comice pears, cored

4 cups watermelon chunks

Strapped for Space?

Small, seedless "personal-sized" watermelons are becoming increasingly available in produce markets for those of you with smaller households or limited refrigerator space.

1. Process the fruits in any order through an electronic juicer according to the manufacturer's directions.

2. Serve alone or over ice.

PER SERVING: Calories: 324 | Fat: 1.3g | Protein: 4.8g | Sodium: 9mg | Carbohydrates: 91g | Sugar: 66g

Apple Plum Juice

The soluble fiber in this juice is terrific for occasional constipation problems, and is rich in vitamins and phytonutrients, too.

INGREDIENTS | YIELDS 1 CUP

2 large apples, cored

4 black plums, pitted

1. Process the fruits in any order through an electronic juicer according to the manufacturer's directions.

2. Serve alone or over ice.

PER SERVING: Calories: 227 | Fat: 1g | Protein: 2.4g | Sodium: 0mg | Carbohydrates: 58g | Sugar: 58g

Fig Heaven

Fresh figs are valuable for controlling hypertension and lowering blood sugar. And of course, the ancient Romans always included them at their banquets as essential to good digestion!

INGREDIENTS | YIELDS 1½ CUPS

10 fresh figs, halved

½ cup pomegranate seeds, white pith removed

1 cup honeydew melon chunks

1. Process the figs through an electronic juicer according to the manufacturer's directions.

2. Add the pomegranate seeds, followed by the melon.

3. Whisk or shake the juice to combine the ingredients and serve alone or over ice.

PER SERVING: Calories: 503 | Fat: 2.5g | Protein: 6g | Sodium: 38mg | Carbohydrates: 127g | Sugar: 106g

More about Figs

Fresh figs are rich in polyphenolic flavonoid antioxidants such ascarotenes, lutein, tannins, and chlorogenic acid. Their antioxidant value is comparable to that of apples.

Crasberry Juice

Apples, raspberries, and cranberries combine in this tart and tempting refresher.

INGREDIENTS | YIELDS 1 CUP

2 apples, cored
1 cup raspberries
1 cup fresh cranberries
Raw honey to taste, if desired

Cranberries—Not Just for Thanksgiving Anymore

Though they make their appearance in markets right around Thanksgiving, fresh cranberries are available throughout the autumn. Indulge in a few bags and freeze them, with no loss of nutritional value.

1. Process the apples through an electronic juicer according to the manufacturer's directions.

2. Add the raspberries and cranberries. Taste the juice and add the honey if desired.

3. Whisk or shake the juice to combine the ingredients and serve alone or over ice.

PER SERVING: Calories: 264 | Fat: 1.3g | Protein: 2.7g | Sodium: 3mg | Carbohydrates: 67g | Sugar: 41g

Cranberry Pear Cocktail

Delish! Tart cranberries are perfectly offset by the milder, sweetness of pears, while ginger adds a spicy note.

INGREDIENTS | YIELDS 1 CUP

3 Anjou pears, cored
1 cup fresh or frozen cranberries
1 (½-inch) piece fresh ginger
Dash of cinnamon

1. Process the pears through an electronic juicer according to the manufacturer's directions.

2. Add the cranberries, followed by the ginger. Add the cinnamon to the resulting juice.

3. Whisk or shake the juice to combine the ingredients and serve alone or over ice.

PER SERVING: Calories: 322 | Fat: 1g | Protein: 2.5g | Sodium: 8mg | Carbohydrates: 84g | Sugar: 47g

The Other Berries

Mulberries are an excellent source of iron, which is a rare feature among berries, while gooseberries, like its cousin the currant, have significantly high amounts of the phenolic phytochemicals that have been found to have beneficial effects against cancer, aging, inflammation, and neurological diseases.

INGREDIENTS | YIELDS 1½ CUPS

2 cups mulberries
2 cups gooseberries

Mulberries

Scientific studies have shown that consumption of mulberries have potential health effects against cancer, aging and neurological diseases, inflammation, diabetes, and bacterial infections. Although more than 100 species of mulberries exist, the top three are the white mulberry, native to eastern and central China; the red or American mulberry, native to the eastern United States; and the black mulberry, native to western Asia.

1. Process the berries through an electronic juicer according to the manufacturer's directions.

2. Mix the juice to combine the ingredients and serve alone or over ice.

PER SERVING: Calories: 264 | Fat: 3.4g | Protein: 5.2g | Sodium: 6mg | Carbohydrates: 61g | Sugar: 48g

Peachy Keen

*Peaches, honeydew melon, and kiwi combine in this
cool summer refresher.*

INGREDIENTS | YIELDS 2 CUPS

3 large peaches, pitted

4 kiwi fruits

2 cups honeydew melon chunks, peeled
and seeded

A Honey of a Melon

Though not as rich in nutrients as cantaloupe, honeydew melon supplies thiamine,
niacin, pantothenic acid, folate, and vitamin
B$_6$, all of which are important for metabolism. Their high water content and subtle
flavor makes them an excellent choice for
combining with other fruits for juicing.

1. Process the peaches through an electronic juicer
   according to the manufacturer's directions.

2. Add the kiwis, followed by the melon.

3. Whisk or shake the juice to combine the ingredients
   and serve alone or over ice.

PER SERVING: Calories: 459 | Fat: 2.5g | Protein: 8.3g |
Sodium: 76mg | Carbohydrates: 113g | Sugar: 60g

Heirloom Tomato Juice

Tomatoes are indeed a fruit and are available in many low-acid heirloom varieties. Combine them with other fruit treasures for a great tasting juice!

INGREDIENTS | YIELDS 2 CUPS

3 heirloom tomatoes, such as Yellow Pear or Cherokee Purple

2 sweet heirloom apples, such as Lady Sweet or Gala, cored

Heirlooms

The resurgence of interest in heirloom varieties of fruits and vegetables has largely come about with the interest in locally grown foods. Commercial farming tends to erode varietals because of its emphasis on consistency. But heirloom varietals are essential, because they frequently have distinct regional characteristics in their ability to withstand climate conditions, pests, and diseases specific to different areas.

1. Process the tomatoes through an electronic juicer according to the manufacturer's directions.

2. Add the apples.

3. Whisk or shake the juice to combine the ingredients and serve alone or over ice.

PER SERVING: Calories: 220 | Fat: 1g | Protein: 4g | Sodium: 18mg | Carbohydrates: 55g | Sugar: 42g

Ugli Fruit Juice

Ugli fruit, native to Jamaica, gets its name from the unattractive pockmarked, thick skin. Ugli fruits range in color from pale green to dark orange. They are similar in size to a grapefruit and shaped like a pear. The citrusy flavor lends itself to juicing and has been a Jamaican favorite for hundreds of years.

INGREDIENTS | YIELDS 2 CUPS

2 ugli fruit, peeled and segmented

Ugli Fruit

Ugli fruit can be cultivated or grown wild. It is said it comes from the accidental crossing of a Seville orange, a tangerine, and grapefruit, so be careful where you spit your seeds! An excellent source of vitamin C, ugli fruit also promotes oral health and fights cardiovascular disease. Some sources indicate it also protects against kidney stone formation.

1. Process the fruits through an electronic juicer according to the manufacturer's directions.

2. Serve immediately.

PER SERVING: Calories: 180 | Fat: 0g | Protein: 4g | Sodium: 0mg | Carbohydrates: 44g | Sugar: 32g

Three-Grape Juice

When it comes to fruit juicing, little can compare with plain old grapes! This trio provides a nice balance of flavor as the white and red grapes balance the more intense Concords.

INGREDIENTS | YIELDS 1½ CUPS

1 cup Concord grapes
1 cup red globe grapes
1 cup white or green seedless grapes

Great Grapes

Regarded in many cultures as "the queen of fruits," grapes are incredibly rich in phytonutrients, antioxidants, vitamins, and minerals and are a rich source of micronutrient minerals like copper, iron, and manganese.

1. Process the grapes in any order through an electronic juicer according to the manufacturer's directions.

2. Serve alone or over ice.

PER SERVING: Calories: 312 | Fat: 0.7g | Protein: 3.2g | Sodium: 9mg | Carbohydrates: 81g | Sugar: 70g

Pineapple Grape Juice

Sweet and satisfying, this recipe contains nutrients that are believed to especially benefit the skin and can even help prevent sunburn!

INGREDIENTS | YIELDS 1½ CUPS

1 cup pineapple chunks
1 bunch red grapes

1. Process the pineapple and the grapes through an electronic juicer according to the manufacturer's directions.

2. Stir the juice to combine the ingredients and serve over ice.

PER SERVING: Calories: 290 | Fat: 0.6g | Protein: 3g | Sodium: 7mg | Carbohydrates: 76g | Sugar: 63g

Guava Jive

The more you eat of the ripened guava or its freshly extracted juice, the more health benefits you gain. Experts know the reddish-fleshed guava contains more nutrients than the white, so extract your juice from the pinkish or reddish-fleshed guava.

INGREDIENTS | YIELDS 1½ CUPS

2 guavas, peeled
1 cup watermelon chunks
2 cups pineapple chunks

Choosing Guava

Guavas, like melons, smell fresh and fruity when they are ripe. Choose fruit that is heavy for its size.

1. Process the guava through an electronic juicer according to the manufacturer's directions.

2. Add the watermelon, followed by the pineapple.

3. Mix the juice to combine the ingredients and serve over ice.

PER SERVING: Calories: 285 | Fat: 1.6g | Protein: 5.5g | Sodium: 7mg | Carbohydrates: 70g | Sugar: 51g

Kiwi Apple Juice

Kiwis have the added benefit of removing excess sodium from the body.

INGREDIENTS | YIELDS 1 CUP

2 medium red apples, cored
3 kiwis

1. Process the apples through an electronic juicer according to manufacturer's directions.

2. Add the kiwi.

3. Mix the juice and serve immediately.

PER SERVING: Calories: 244 | Fat: 1.2g | Protein: 2.8g | Sodium: 11mg | Carbohydrates: 61g | Sugar: 22g

Black and Blue

Two great berries combine in one fine juice. In addition to their antioxidant benefits, these berries are also believed to have a beneficial effect on mood.

INGREDIENTS | YIELDS 1 CUP

1 cup blueberries
1 cup blackberries
¼ lemon, peeled

1. Process the berries and lemon though your juicer according to the manufacturer's directions.

2. Serve the juice alone or over ice.

PER SERVING: Calories: 150 | Fat: 1.2g | Protein: 3.2g | Sodium: 3.2mg | Carbohydrates: 36g | Sugar: 22g

Lemon-Lime Ade

A classic that will have you wanting to set up your own sidewalk stand!

INGREDIENTS | YIELDS 1½ CUPS

3 lemons, peeled
6 Mexican limes
1 tablespoon raw honey
6 ounces water

1. Process the lemons and limes through an electronic juicer according to the manufacturer's directions.

2. Add the honey and the water to the juice and stir to combine.

3. Serve over ice.

PER SERVING: Calories: 235 | Fat: 1.3g | Protein: 4.7g | Sodium: 12mg | Carbohydrates: 76g | Sugar: 28g

Honey Orange Dew

This juice is a great source of vitamin C. Honeydew melons are available year-round. When they are perfectly ripe, the skin is wrinkled.

INGREDIENTS | YIELDS 1½ CUPS

½ honeydew melon, peeled

½ cup watermelon, peeled

½ orange, peeled

Vitamins to the Rescue

Research shows that many antioxidants interact with and protect each other. Vitamin C, for instance, can react with a damaged vitamin E molecule and convert it back to its antioxidant form, while the antioxidant glutathione can return vitamin C to its original form. Studies also show that vitamin C enhances the protective effects of vitamin E.

1. Process the melons and orange though an electronic juicer according to the manufacturer's directions.

2. Serve the juice alone or over ice.

PER SERVING: Calories: 233 | Fat: 0.8g | Protein: 3.7g | Sodium: 90mg | Carbohydrates: 58g | Sugar: 51g

CHAPTER 10

Junior Juices

No doubt about it, kids love juice! Even the pickiest eaters can get greedy when it comes to a wholesome, healthful glass of fresh juice, so don't deprive them of all the benefits they need to build strong bodies. While experts recommend that babies and toddlers should avoid unpasteurized juices in favor of mother's milk, older children can enjoy a myriad of benefits even if they don't know it's "good for them."

Kid-Friendly Juices

Here are some rules to keep in mind when juicing for and with your kids. First, keep it simple. Don't come at them with too many complex flavors and don't think you can sneak in kale or turnips without them suspecting something. Those are strong flavors even for adults. Second, keep all flavors subtle and on the mild side. Bean sprouts, for example, have very little flavor but all the nutrition your child needs, even if they won't touch green beans on the plate. Sweeten them up with an apple or some grapes and you'll likely be more successful in your quest to get your vegetable hater some necessary nutrients. Third, dilute fresh juices with filtered water. Children's digestive systems are more delicate, and some may be prone to allergies or sensitivities to untried foods. Just as some adults need time for their systems to adjust to fresh juice, so do kids, so take it easy. Fourth, NEVER put any child under the age of twelve on a juice fast. Developing systems and child-sized metabolisms are more easily thrown out of whack when too much of an emphasis is placed on one food group or another.

Finally, keep it fun. Ask them to help dream up their own imaginative combinations, and give your juices silly or kid-friendly names. Most children are far more likely to sample something called Green Goblin Juice than they are to try a Chlorophyll Cocktail.

Juices Fit for a Kid

Pumpkin Punch

*Your Harry Potter fans will be delighted to learn
that there really is a pumpkin juice, just like in the books!*

**INGREDIENTS | YIELDS 1 CUP
(2 SERVINGS)**

½ cup fresh pumpkin chunks
1 carrot, trimmed
1 orange, peeled
¼ teaspoon pumpkin pie spice

1. Process the pumpkin and carrot through an electronic juicer according to the manufacturer's directions.

2. Add the orange. Add the pie spice to the resulting juice.

3. Stir the juice to blend and dilute with ½ cup water or skim milk.

PER SERVING: Calories: 106 | Fat: 0.3g | Protein: 2.4 | Sodium: 50mg | Carbohydrates: 26g | Sugar: 16g

Apple Fantastic

For kids' juice, milder apples like Delicious or Baldwin will do just fine.

**INGREDIENTS | YIELDS 1½ CUPS
(3 SERVINGS)**

4 Delicious or Golden Delicious apples, cored
½ cup filtered water

1. Process the apples through an electronic juicer according to the manufacturer's directions.

2. Dilute with water and mix.

PER SERVING: Calories: 164 | Fat: 0.5g | Protein: 0.8g | Sodium: 3.3mg | Carbohydrates: 46g | Sugar: 34g

Variation

If your kids flatly refuse anything but their favorite apple juice, try adding just a few grapes or a bit of melon, a little at a time, until they get accustomed to the variation in flavor.

White Grape Wonder

This juice provides wonderful nutrition and doesn't stain kids' clothes like some other grape juices can.

INGREDIENTS | YIELDS 1½ CUPS (3 SERVINGS)

2 cups white or green seedless grapes
½ cup filtered water

1. Process the grapes through an electronic juicer according to the manufacturer's directions.

2. Dilute with water and mix.

PER SERVING: Calories: 208 | Fat: 0.4g | Protein: 2g | Sodium: 6mg | Carbohydrates: 54g | Sugar: 46g

Green Goblin Juice

Pronounced grape flavor and great green color. They'll never suspect there's spinach in there!

INGREDIENTS | YIELDS 2 CUPS (4 SERVINGS)

2 cups white or green seedless grapes
½ cup fresh spinach
1 cup filtered water

1. Process the grapes through an electronic juicer according to the manufacturer's directions.

2. Add the spinach.

3. Dilute with water and mix.

PER SERVING: Calories: 211 | Fat: 0.5g | Protein: 2.6g | Sodium: 17mg | Carbohydrates: 55g | Sugar: 46g

Watermelon Mix

Kids love watermelon, and the addition of a few cherries only makes it better!

**INGREDIENTS | YIELDS 2 CUPS
(4 SERVINGS)**

2 cups watermelon chunks
½ cup sweet cherries, pitted
1 cup filtered water

1. Process the watermelon through an electronic juicer according to the manufacturer's directions.

2. Add the cherries.

3. Dilute with water and mix.

PER SERVING: Calories: 139 | Fat: 0.6g | Protein: 2.6g | Sodium: 3mg | Carbohydrates: 35g | Sugar: 28g

Kiwi Pear Potion

This juice is especially great in cold and flu season to arm your little ones with extra vitamin C.

**INGREDIENTS | YIELDS 1 CUP
(2 SERVINGS)**

2 kiwi fruit
2 pears, cored
½ cup water or skim milk

1. Process the kiwi through an electronic juicer according to the manufacturer's directions.

2. Add the pears.

3. Dilute with water or skim milk and mix.

PER SERVING: Calories: 264 | Fat: 1g | Protein: 2.6g | Sodium: 10mg | Carbohydrates: 68g | Sugar: 29g

Mighty Grape

An old standby with a new twist—mellow honeydew melon.

INGREDIENTS | YIELDS 1 CUP (2 SERVINGS)

1 cup Concord grapes
1 cup honeydew melon
½ cup water

1. Process the grapes through an electronic juicer according to the manufacturer's directions.

2. Add the melon.

3. Dilute with water to taste and serve.

PER SERVING: Calories: 165 | Fat: 0.5g | Protein: 2g | Sodium: 33mg | Carbohydrates: 42g | Sugar: 37g

Apple Grape Magic

Perennial favorites in kidland, this combination is a guaranteed winner with the younger set.

INGREDIENTS | YIELDS 1 CUP (2 SERVINGS)

1 cup Concord grapes
2 apples, cored
½ cup water

1. Process the grapes through an electronic juicer according to the manufacturer's directions.

2. Add the apples.

3. Dilute with water to taste.

PER SERVING: Calories: 209 | Fat: 0.5g | Protein: 1.6g | Sodium: 3mg | Carbohydrates: 55g | Sugar: 45g

OJ Fooler

*Imagine their faces when you ask them to taste,
and then tell them there aren't any oranges in this one!*

**INGREDIENTS | YIELDS 1 CUP
(2 SERVINGS)**

3 or 4 tangerines or clementines, peeled
½ cup water

Easy on the Tummy
Tangerines or clementines have just as
much nutrition and vitamin C as oranges,
but are friendlier for younger kids, who
may be sensitive to an orange's higher acid
content.

1. Process the fruit through an electronic juicer according
   to the manufacturer's directions.

2. Dilute with water to taste.

PER SERVING: Calories: 139 | Fat: 0.8g | Protein: 2g |
Sodium: 5mg | Carbohydrates: 35g | Sugar: 27g

Apple Pie

Juice for dessert? Why not? A great way to introduce kids to juicing is by substituting juice for dessert after meals.

INGREDIENTS | YIELDS 1½ CUPS (3 SERVINGS)

2 apples, cored
8 stalks celery, with leaves
Dash of cinnamon

1. Process the apples and celery through an electronic juicer according to the manufacturer's directions.

2. Add the cinnamon to the resulting juice.

3. Mix the juice to combine the ingredients and serve.

PER SERVING: Calories: 52 | Fat: 0.2g | Protein: 0.9g | Sodium: 85mg | Carbohydrates: 12g | Sugar: 9g

Apple Watermelon Shake

Kids who play hard need hydration, especially in the summer, and this one's a great choice.

INGREDIENTS | YIELDS 1½ CUPS (3 SERVINGS)

2 apples, cored
3 cups watermelon chunks

1. Process fruit through an electronic juicer according to the manufacturer's directions.

2. Shake the juice together with ice and serve.

PER SERVING: Calories: 80 | Fat: 0.3g | Protein: 1g | Sodium: 1.5mg | Carbohydrates: 20g | Sugar: 16g

Plain Pear

An excellent choice for toddlers, this one is just right for a sippy cup.

**INGREDIENTS | YIELDS 1 CUP
(2 SERVINGS)**

2 pears, cored
½ cup filtered water

Make Your Own

Kids are likely to enjoy their juice more when you let them pick their own combinations. Simply put an array of prepared fruits and veggies out on the table and let them make their choices.

1. Process the pears through an electronic juicer according to the manufacturer's directions.

2. Dilute with water and serve.

PER SERVING: Calories: 85 | Fat: 0.1g | Protein: 0.5g | Sodium: 1.4mg | Carbohydrates: 22g | Sugar: 14g

Mint Shake

Sweet and minty. Most kids love the minty flavor, and will never suspect the chlorophyll and phytonutrients this juice contains.

**INGREDIENTS | YIELDS 1 CUP
(2 SERVINGS)**

2 cups pineapple chunks
½ cup fresh mint
½ cup filtered water or skim milk

Pineapple Sensitivity

Very young kids can have sensitivity to fresh pineapple, but you can use canned, packed in its own juice.

1. Process the pineapple through an electronic juicer according to the manufacturer's directions.

2. Roll the mint into a ball and add to the juicer.

3. Dilute the juice with water or milk, and shake until foamy.

PER SERVING: Calories: 95 | Fat: 0.3g | Protein: 1.6g | Sodium: 8mg | Carbohydrates: 23g | Sugar: 16g

Bunny Juice

Everyone knows that bunnies love carrots, right? This one will teach your little one to love them, too.

INGREDIENTS | YIELDS 1 CUP (2 SERVINGS)

3 carrots, trimmed

1 Gala apple, cored

Process the carrots and apples through an electronic juicer according to the manufacturer's directions and serve.

PER SERVING: Calories: 70 | Fat: 0.3g | Protein: 1g | Sodium: 74mg | Carbohydrates: 17g | Sugar: 10g

Green Slime Super Juice

There are times when a little reverse psychology works wonders when it comes to getting kids to try new things. Call it slime and dare them to try it—they'll like it!

INGREDIENTS | YIELDS 1½ CUPS (3 SERVINGS)

1½ cups collard greens

1 lemon, peeled

2 tablespoons agave nectar

Agave Nectar

Agave nectar has become a popular alternative to artificial sweeteners, because it has little impact on blood sugar.

1. Process the collard greens through an electronic juicer according to the manufacturer's directions.

2. Add the lemon.

3. Stir the juice to combine the ingredients and sweeten with the agave nectar.

PER SERVING: Calories: 53 | Fat: 0.1g | Protein: 0.6g | Sodium: 4.5mg | Carbohydrates: 14g | Sugar: 12g

Honey Melon Juice

*This delicious juice is high in vitamins C and B_2,
which strengthen immunity—plus kids love it!*

**INGREDIENTS | YIELDS 3 CUPS
(6 SERVINGS)**

½ honeydew melon, peeled and seeded
1 cup black grapes
½ medium seedless watermelon, cut into chunks
1 cup low-fat milk

1. Process the honeydew through an electronic juicer according to the manufacturer's directions.

2. Add the grapes, followed by the watermelon.

3. Combine the juice with the milk and serve.

PER SERVING: Calories: 177 | Fat: 1g | Protein: 4g |
Sodium: 37mg | Carbohydrates: 42g | Sugar: 36g

Spapple Juice

Just call it that; they'll never suspect the spinach.

**INGREDIENTS | YIELDS 1 CUP
(2 SERVINGS)**

1 cup spinach
2 Gala or Pink Lady apples, cored
1 lemon, peeled
3 or 4 drops stevia (optional)

1. Process the spinach through an electronic juicer according to the manufacturer's directions.

2. Add the apples and the lemon.

3. Sweeten the juice with stevia as desired.

PER SERVING: Calories: 64 | Fat: 0.2g | Protein: 1g |
Sodium: 12mg | Carbohydrates: 17g | Sugar: 11g

Stevia

Stevia is popular sweetener used in place of sugar or artificial sweeteners. It's available as an extract or in powdered form. It comes from an herb in the sunflower family.

Peppermint Juice

In addition to great flavor, peppermint is a great natural cure for upset tummies.

INGREDIENTS | YIELDS 1½ CUPS (3 SERVINGS)

½ cup fresh peppermint leaves
½ cucumber
½ cup bean sprouts
2 leaves romaine lettuce
1 teaspoon raw honey (optional)

1. Process the peppermint and cucumber through an electronic juicer according to the manufacturer's directions.

2. Add the sprouts and the lettuce.

3. Sweeten the juice with honey as desired.

PER SERVING: Calories: 26 | Fat: 0.3g | Protein: 2.3g | Sodium: 8.8mg | Carbohydrates: 5g | Sugar: 1g

Jungle Juice

*When busy kids don't have time to eat,
this juice will keep them going.*

INGREDIENTS | YIELDS 3 CUPS (6 SERVINGS)

¼ cup fresh mint
1 pineapple, peeled and cut into chunks
1 papaya, peeled and seeded
1 small mango, peeled and seeded

1. Process the fruits in any order through an electronic juicer according to the manufacturer's directions.

2. Mix the juice to combine the ingredients and serve.

PER SERVING: Calories: 119 | Fat: 0.3g | Protein: 1.4g | Sodium: 4.8mg | Carbohydrates: 30g | Sugar: 22g

Kid's Choice

*Mild melon, juicy cherries, and grapes make for great taste and
a really appealing color in this combination.*

**INGREDIENTS | YIELDS 1½ CUPS
(3 SERVINGS)**

1 cup cantaloupe chunks
½ cup sweet cherries, pitted
1 cup white or green seedless grapes

1. Process the fruits in any order through an electronic juicer according to the manufacturer's directions.

2. Mix the juice to combine the ingredients and serve.

PER SERVING: Calories: 68 | Fat: 0.2g | Protein: 1g |
Sodium: 9mg | Carbohydrates: 17g | Sugar: 15g

Purple Moo Juice

If your child is allergic to dairy, use soy or rice milk instead.

**INGREDIENTS | YIELDS 1½ CUPS
(3 SERVINGS)**

1 cup blueberries
½ cup blackberries
1 cup skim milk or soy milk

1. Process the berries through an electronic juicer according to the manufacturer's directions.

2. Mix the juice with the milk to combine and serve.

PER SERVING: Calories: 72 | Fat: 1g | Protein: 3.4g |
Sodium: 36mg | Carbohydrates: 13g | Sugar: 10g

Soy Milk

As an alternative to dairy, soy milk is also a good source of copper, vitamin D, riboflavin, vitamin B_{12}, and calcium.

Joy Juice

A winning combo that tastes like fruit, but sneaks in a cucumber for good measure.

**INGREDIENTS | YIELDS 3 CUPS
(6 SERVINGS)**

1 small seedless watermelon, peeled and cubed

1 medium cucumber

1 large lime, or medium lemon, peeled

1. Process the watermelon and cucumber through an electronic juicer according to the manufacturer's directions.

2. Add the lime.

3. Stir the juice to combine the ingredients and serve.

PER SERVING: Calories: 236 | Fat: 1.2g | Protein: 4.9g | Sodium: 9mg | Carbohydrates: 59g | Sugar: 47g

Bedtime Snack

If your child is hyper at bedtime, try this lettuce-based juice for a calming effect.

**INGREDIENTS | YIELDS 1 CUP
(2 SERVINGS)**

1 cup chopped romaine or iceberg lettuce

1 apple, cored

Process the lettuce and apple through your juicer according to the manufacturer's directions and serve.

PER SERVING: Calories: 30 | Fat: 0.1g | Protein: 0.4g | Sodium: 1.8mg | Carbohydrates: 7.7g | Sugar: 5.8g

Orangeberry Juice

*This juice contains an array of nutrients to give kids energy,
making it an excellent breakfast juice.*

**INGREDIENTS | YIELDS 1½ CUPS
(3 SERVINGS)**

1 cup fresh raspberries

2 oranges, peeled

2 nectarines, pitted

Oranges and Calcium

Just one of the reasons orange-based juice is important for kids is that the calcium they contain helps build strong bones. A medium-sized orange has 52 mg of calcium.

1. Process the raspberries and oranges through an electronic juicer according to the manufacturer's directions.

2. Add the nectarines.

3. Whisk or shake the juice and serve alone or diluted with ½ cup skim milk.

PER SERVING: Calories: 89 | Fat: 0.6g | Protein: 2g | Sodium: 0.41mg | Carbohydrates: 21g | Sugar: 14g

Mango Pear Punch

Yummy! The pears nicely offset the sharper notes of mango here in a way that's sure to please the less than sophisticated kiddie palate.

INGREDIENTS | YIELDS 1½ CUPS (3 SERVINGS)

2 small mangoes, seeded
2 medium pears, cored
2 medium carrots, trimmed
2 medium apples, cored

Kid-Sized Portions

While older kids can handle a full serving of undiluted fresh juice, reduce portion size for young ones, limiting servings to ½ to ¾ cup. Too much more than that can lead to stomach or gastrointestinal upset.

1. Process the mangoes through an electronic juicer according to the manufacturer's directions.

2. Add the pears, followed by the carrots.

3. Add the apples.

4. Mix the juice to combine the ingredients and serve.

PER SERVING: Calories: 226 | Fat: 0.7g | Protein: 1.8g | Sodium: 32mg | Carbohydrates: 59g | Sugar: 44g

CHAPTER 11

The Juice Doctor

Though there's a world of documentation out there to support juicing's beneficial effects on overall health and well-being, when it to comes to claims of miracle "cures" or recovery from devastating and debilitating conditions, it's important to be aware of the facts and consult with your personal physician or health care professional before embarking on a juicing "cure."

Juice Is a Powerful Weapon

There's no doubt about it: Simple dietary adjustments, such as adding fresh fruit and vegetable juices to your routine, can do you a world of good. Scientists discover new benefits about the enzymes, vitamins, and micronutrients available through juicing all the time. We know that certain fruits and vegetables can help regulate blood pressure, control blood sugar, and even retard the growth of cancer cells. Many people report being able to throw away prescription medications after a long-term juicing regimen. But all by itself, juicing can't be considered a "cure" for disease. It is instead a powerful weapon in your arsenal when it comes to disease prevention, simply because a combination of nutrients, antioxidants, and minerals aid the body in a holistic way. Juice doesn't target disease—it simply makes vital nutrients available to your entire system.

Therefore, if you have medical problems such as diabetes, cancer, high blood pressure, arthritis, or any of the other problems for which certain juices are recommend, the first and most important step is to remain proactive in your own care, and to monitor your progress under professional advice. Let your body be your guide and both you and your doctor will doubtless be pleased with the results.

Juices to Preserve and Protect Your Health

Salty Dog

Considered especially beneficial for those with type 2 diabetes. Beta cells within the pancreas produce insulin, and cucumbers help to increase the hormone required by the beta cells in insulin production.

INGREDIENTS | YIELDS 1 CUP

2 cucumbers
1 lemon, peeled
1 (¼-inch) piece fresh ginger
Pinch of kosher or sea salt

Grains of Salt

It's always a good idea to substitute kosher or sea salt in your recipes. Neither contain additives, and they have lower sodium overall than commercial table salt.

1. Process the cucumbers and lemon through your juicer according to the manufacturer's directions.

2. Add the ginger.

3. Add salt to the juice according to your taste.

4. Serve alone or over ice.

PER SERVING: Calories: 125 | Fat: 1g | Protein: 5g | Sodium: 309mg | Carbohydrates: 31g | Sugar: 11g

Cauli-Carrot Combo

This combination of vegetable juices is a tasty choice for diabetics who steer clear of sugary juices.

INGREDIENTS | YIELDS 1½ CUPS

1 cup cauliflower florets
3 carrots, trimmed
1 celery stalk, with leaves

1. Process the cauliflowers and carrots through your juicer according to the manufacturer's directions.

2. Add the celery.

3. Serve the juice alone or over ice.

PER SERVING: Calories: 119 | Fat: 0.8g | Protein: 4.2g | Sodium: 211mg | Carbohydrates: 26g | Sugar: 12g

Cabbage Patch Combo

The great thing about cabbage, aside from its health benefits,
is that it's inexpensive year-round.

INGREDIENTS | YIELDS 1½ CUPS

¼ head red cabbage
1 cup green cabbage
2 large apples, cored

1. Process the cabbages through your juicer according to the manufacturer's directions.

2. Add the apples.

3. Stir the juice to combine the ingredients. Serve alone or over ice.

PER SERVING: Calories: 281 | Fat: 0.8g | Protein: 4.9g | Sodium: 53mg | Carbohydrates: 72g | Sugar: 53g

Asparagus Zucchini Medley

There's nothing better than asparagus for regulating blood sugar levels.

INGREDIENTS | YIELDS 1½ CUPS

8 stalks asparagus, trimmed
2 medium zucchini, trimmed

1. Process the vegetables through your juicer according to the manufacturer's directions.

2. Mix the juice to combine the ingredients and serve over ice.

PER SERVING: Calories: 92 | Fat: 1.4g | Protein: 7.5g | Sodium: 33mg | Carbohydrates: 17g | Sugar: 12g

Brussels Bean Juice

*Brussels sprouts and beans are both good sources of natural insulin,
and so are considered beneficial for people with diabetes and pre-diabetes.*

INGREDIENTS | YIELDS 1 CUP

1 cup green beans

6 Brussels sprouts

1 lemon, peeled

Turning Up Your Nose?

The stronger flavors of cabbages and Brussels sprouts are greatly mitigated by the lemon juice.

1. Process the beans through an electronic juicer according to the manufacturer's directions.

2. Add the Brussels sprouts, followed by the lemon.

3. Mix the juice to combine the ingredients. Serve alone or over ice.

PER SERVING: Calories: 99 | Fat: 0.7g | Protein: 6.5g | Sodium: 36mg | Carbohydrates: 23g | Sugar: 7.5g

7-Up

These seven ingredients combine in a powerful vegetable juice for cancer prevention because of their ability to fight free radicals and inflammation.

INGREDIENTS | YIELDS 1½ CUPS

3 tomatoes
2 medium carrots, trimmed
1 celery stalk, leaves intact
½ cup parsley
2 green onions
1 cup cauliflower florets
2 cloves garlic, peeled

1. Process the tomatoes through an electronic juicer according to the manufacturer's directions.

2. Add the carrots, celery, and parsley.

3. Next add the onions, the cauliflower, and the garlic.

4. Mix the juice to combine the ingredients. Serve alone or over ice.

PER SERVING: Calories: 183 | Fat: 1.8g | Protein: 8.2g | Sodium: 201mg | Carbohydrates: 39g | Sugar: 20g

Cancer Fighter 1

*When it comes to fighting or preventing cancer remember the
four Cs—collards, cabbage, carrots, and cauliflower.*

INGREDIENTS | YIELDS 1½ CUPS

1 cup chopped collard greens
1 cup chopped cabbage
1 cup cauliflower florets
2 carrots, trimmed

The Right Stuff

Cabbage and cauliflower contain several chemical compounds that research indicates provides protection against cancer. One of these, indole-3-carbinol, may deactivate estrogen and reduce the risk of breast cancer, while the compound sulforaphane helps degrade free radicals and some carcinogenic substances.

1. Process the greens through an electronic juicer according to the manufacturer's directions.

2. Add the cabbage and cauliflower, followed by the carrots.

3. Mix the juice to combine the ingredients. Serve alone or over ice.

PER SERVING: Calories: 94 | Fat: 0.7g | Protein: 4.6g | Sodium: 118mg | Carbohydrates: 20g | Sugar: 9g

Cancer Fighter 2

Wheatgrass juice contains thirteen vitamins. The chlorophyll and beta-carotene in wheatgrass juice is beneficial in fighting and preventing cancer.

INGREDIENTS | YIELDS 1½ CUPS

1 beet, greens included
1 cup cauliflower florets
1 carrot, trimmed
½ cup wheatgrass

Wheatgrass Tip
To derive maximum juice and benefit from wheatgrass, use a masticating juicer.

1. Process the beet and its greens through an electronic juicer according to the manufacturer's directions.

2. Add the cauliflower, followed by the carrot and the wheatgrass.

3. Mix the juice to combine the ingredients. Serve alone or over ice.

PER SERVING: Calories: 125 | Fat: 0.5g | Protein: 5g | Sodium: 143g | Carbohydrates: 19g | Sugar: 10g

Strawberry Papaya Juice

Thought to be beneficial in reducing the risk of colon cancer. The soluble fiber in papaya is able to bind itself with cancer-causing toxins in the colon and aids in their elimination.

INGREDIENTS | YIELDS 1 CUP

1 cup strawberries
1 papaya, seeded
1 cup cantaloupe chunks

1. Process the berries and the papaya through an electronic juicer according to the manufacturer's directions.

2. Add the cantaloupe.

3. Stir the juice, and enjoy alone or over ice.

PER SERVING: Calories: 153 | Fat: 1g | Protein: 3g | Sodium: 27mg | Fiber: 7g | Carbohydrates: 37g | Sugar: 27g

Green Power

These dark leafy greens are rich in carotenoids, a specific group of antioxidants.

INGREDIENTS | YIELDS 1 CUP

1 cup spinach
½ cup kale
3 large leaves romaine lettuce
1 cup mustard greens

1. Process the greens through an electronic juicer according to the manufacturer's directions.

2. Stir the juice to combine the ingredients and serve over ice.

PER SERVING: Calories: 52 | Fat: 0.7g | Protein: 4.5g | Sodium: 58mg | Carbohydrates: 10g | Sugar: 2g

Antioxidants and Free Radicals

Free radicals are elements thought to damage cells, which in turn can lead to the onset of cancerous growths. Antioxidants fight free radicals and reduce the risk of cellular damage.

Power PAC

Proanthocyanidins (or PACs) are powerful cancer fighters and are found in beets, blueberries, and grapes as well as some other foods.

INGREDIENTS | YIELDS 1 CUP

1 cup blueberries
1 cup grapes
2 plums, pitted

1. Process the fruits in any order through an electronic juicer according to the manufacturer's directions.

2. Serve immediately.

PER SERVING: Calories: 52 | Fat: 0.7g | Protein: 4.5g | Sodium: 58mg | Carbohydrates: 10g | Sugar: 2g

Beet High Blood Pressure

High blood pressure happens when the flow of blood puts too much pressure on your arteries. Fresh fruits and vegetables have a wonderful effect on lowering blood pressure, and beets are especially effective.

INGREDIENTS | YIELDS 1 CUP

1 medium beet, tailed and trimmed
1 medium carrot, trimmed
3 stalks celery, with leaves

Celery and Blood Pressure

The phthalides in celery have been shown to lower blood pressure. Celery is also a great source of potassium, calcium, and magnesium, each of which help to control hypertension, according to the Linus Pauling Institute.

1. Process the beet through an electronic juicer according to the manufacturer's directions.

2. Add the carrots and the celery.

3. Stir the juice to combine the ingredients. Serve alone or over ice.

PER SERVING: Calories: 74 | Fat: 0.4g | Protein: 2.6g | Sodium: 194mg | Carbohydrates: 16g | Sugar: 10g

Blood Pressure Buster

Science Daily reports that researchers from the London School of Medicine discovered that beet juice can lower blood pressure within an hour of drinking it and keep blood pressure down for up to twenty-four hours.

INGREDIENTS | YIELDS 1 CUP

1 medium beet, tailed and trimmed
1 medium orange, peeled
1 medium apple, cored

1. Process the beet through an electronic juicer according to the manufacturer's directions.

2. Add the orange and the apple.

3. Stir the juice to combine the ingredients. Serve alone or over ice.

PER SERVING: Calories: 133 | Fat: 0.4g | Protein: 2.5g | Sodium: 63mg | Carbohydrates: 33g | Sugar: 25g

Citrus Blend

The fruits in the citrus family can work wonders at reducing high blood pressure.

INGREDIENTS | YIELDS 1 CUP

1 medium orange, peeled
2 limes, peeled
1 lemon, peeled
1 tablespoon raw honey

1. Process the fruits in any order through an electronic juicer according to the manufacturer's directions.

2. Add the honey to the resulting juice.

3. Stir the juice to combine the ingredients. Serve alone or over ice.

PER SERVING: Calories: 166 | Fat: 0.5g | Protein: 2.5g | Sodium: 4.6mg | Carbohydrates: 48g | Sugar: 30g

Citrus and Blood Pressure

Studies suggest that vitamin C reduces systolic blood pressure. A glass of orange juice at every meal can significantly lower your blood pressure. Any citrus fruit will do, but if you are also taking cholesterol medication, check with your doctor before drinking grapefruit juice.

Mellow Melon Juice

Watermelon and cantaloupe, or muskmelon, have been shown to significantly reduce problem blood pressure when consumed regularly.

INGREDIENTS | YIELDS 1 CUP

1 cup watermelon chunks

1 cup cantaloupe chunks

4 or 5 strawberries

1. Process the fruits in any order through an electronic juicer according to the manufacturer's directions.

2. Serve the juice immediately over ice.

PER SERVING: Calories: 114 | Fat: 0.6g | Protein: 2.5g | Sodium: 26mg | Carbohydrates: 27g | Sugar: 24g

Banana Grapefruit Smoothie

The potassium found in bananas is very heart healthy. Make this one in a blender for best results.

INGREDIENTS | YIELDS 1 CUP

1 large pink grapefruit, peeled

1 banana, peeled

½ cup skim milk or coconut water

1. Place the grapefruit sections, the banana, and the milk or coconut water in a blender and purée until smooth.

2. Serve the smoothie immediately.

PER SERVING: Calories: 223 | Fat: 1.7g | Protein: 6.8g | Sodium: 54mg | Carbohydrates: 49g | Sugar: 36g

Blueberry Raspberry Blend

Just as is true for many other areas of health, when it comes to reducing high blood pressure, it's the berries! In addition to their high levels of antioxidants, berries contain flavonoids, which have been found to decrease the risk of hypertension by as much as 25 percent.

INGREDIENTS | YIELDS 1 CUP

1 cup blueberries
1 cup raspberries

Process the berries through your juicer according to the manufacturer's directions. Serve immediately and enjoy!

PER SERVING: Calories: 148 | Fat: 1.2g | Protein: 2.5g | Sodium: 2.7mg | Carbohydrates: 36g | Sugar: 20g

Bok Choy Blend

For those who can't abide cabbage, the milder flavored bok choy is a great substitute. Reducing blood pressure is just one of the many health benefits it has to offer as it also includes antioxidants and vitamin C, and is a rich source of potassium.

INGREDIENTS | YIELDS 1½ CUPS

2 large leaves bok choy
2 stalks celery, with leaves
1 cup spinach
3 leaves romaine lettuce

1. Process the bok choy through your juicer according to the manufacturer's directions.

2. Add the celery, followed by the spinach and the lettuce.

3. Serve the juice alone or over ice.

PER SERVING: Calories: 37 | Fat: 0.5g | Protein: 2.8g | Sodium: 112mg | Carbohydrates: 6.8g | Sugar: 3g

Osteo Juice

*Osteoporosis is a medical condition that results in the weakening of bones.
It primarily affects females, although some males may also experience osteoporosis.
Over half of all American women have some degree of this condition.*

INGREDIENTS | YIELDS 1 CUP

1 cup broccoli florets
1 turnip, including greens
2 green onions
1 cup spinach

Bone Builders

While juicing is not a substitute for medical treatment of osteoporosis, some fruits and veggies are high in both sulphur and magnesium, both of which prevent loss of calcium from the body. They are broccoli, kale, spinach, onions, and turnips; and fruits high in magnesium, such as bananas, cantaloupe, and avocados.

1. Process the broccoli through an electronic juicer according to the manufacturer's directions.

2. Add the turnip and its greens, followed by the onions and the spinach.

3. Stir the juice to combine the ingredients. Serve alone or over ice.

PER SERVING: Calories: 61 | Fat: 0.6g | Protein: 4.2g | Sodium: 98mg | Carbohydrates: 12g | Sugar: 5g

High Calcium Cocktail

For those at risk of osteoporosis, extra calcium never hurts.

INGREDIENTS | YIELDS 1 CUP

1 large orange, peeled
1 tangerine, peeled
2 kiwis

Extra Calcium Needn't Come from Milk

If you're in search of ways to add extra calcium to your diet, consider dried fruits such as apricots, dates, and prunes.

1. Process the fruits in any order through an electronic juicer according to the manufacturer's directions.

2. Stir the juice to combine the ingredients. Serve immediately.

PER SERVING: Calories: 219 | Fat: 1g | Protein: 3.8g | Sodium: 9mg | Carbohydrates: 54g | Sugar: 25g

Super Immunity Booster

*When cold and flu season comes around, this citrus powerhouse
is better than a flu shot!*

INGREDIENTS | YIELDS 2 CUPS

2 medium grapefruits, peeled
2 Valencia oranges, peeled
2 Mineola tangelos, peeled
1 small lime, quartered
2 pomegranates, peeled; white pith removed

1. Process the grapefruit and oranges through an electronic juicer according to the manufacturer's directions.

2. Add the tangeloes and the lime.

3. Add the pomegranate seeds.

4. Stir the juice to combine the ingredients and serve immediately.

PER SERVING: Calories: 636 | Fat: 5.8g | Protein: 12g | Sodium: 14mg | Carbohydrates: 153g | Sugar: 92g

Headache Cure

Try this juice the next time you feel a headache coming on.

INGREDIENTS | YIELDS 1 CUP

¾ cup cantaloupe, cut into chunks
1 (½-inch) piece fresh ginger
2 small key or Mexican limes

1. Process the cantaloupe, ginger, and limes through an electronic juicer according to the manufacturer's directions.

2. Stir the juice to combine the ingredients. Serve alone or over ice.

PER SERVING: Calories: 41 | Fat: 0.2g | Protein: 1g | Sodium: 3mg | Carbohydrates: 14g | Sugar: 2g

Breathe Easy Juice

Vitamin A figures prominently in maintaining healthy lungs. Recent research suggests that not only can vitamin A prevent the occurrence of emphysema, it also might be able to reverse the damage caused by the disease.

INGREDIENTS | YIELDS 1½ CUPS

1 sweet potato, peeled
2 carrots, trimmed
2 cups blackberries

1. Process the sweet potato and carrots through an electronic juicer according to the manufacturer's directions.

2. Add the blackberries.

3. Stir the juice to combine the ingredients. Serve alone or over ice.

PER SERVING: Calories: 276 | Fat: 1.7g | Protein: 6.9g | Sodium: 143mg | Carbohydrates: 63g | Sugar: 24g

Common Cold Ade

Vitamin C helps to alleviate cold symptoms.

INGREDIENTS | YIELDS 1½ CUPS

2 oranges, peeled
3 leaves rainbow chard
½ lemon, peeled

1. Process the oranges and the chard through an electronic juicer according to the manufacturer's directions.

2. Add the lemon.

3. Mix the juice to combine the ingredients. Serve alone or over ice.

PER SERVING: Calories: 158 | Fat: 0.6g | Protein: 5.3g | Sodium: 307mg | Carbohydrates: 38g | Sugar: 26g

Happiness in a Glass

Pineapple contains manganese and thiamine,
which when metabolized translate to increased energy and higher spirits.

INGREDIENTS | YIELDS 1½ CUPS

1 cup pineapple chunks
2 cups grapes

All about Iron

Iron is such an important mineral because it transports life-sustaining nutrients throughout the body. It also increases oxygen in the blood while removing carbon dioxide. Iron ensures a healthy immune system and creates energy. Iron deficiency can cause a variety of health problems including fatigue, irritability, and headaches.

1. Process the fruits through an electronic juicer according to the manufacturer's directions.

2. Stir the juice to combine the ingredients. Serve alone or over ice.

PER SERVING: Calories: 290 | Fat: 0.6g | Protein: 3g | Sodium: 7.6mg | Carbohydrates: 76g | Sugar: 63g

Combat Depression

For some, seasonal depression can be a problem, for others it can result from external stressors. In any event, these foods, when juiced, can provide a healthy lift when you're battling the blues.

INGREDIENTS | YIELDS 1 CUP

4 broccoli spears
½ cup spinach leaves
3 Swiss chard leaves
1 red bell pepper, seeded

Look to the B Group for Treating Mood

Folic acid, or folate, as well as increasing and maintaining levels of B vitamins in the blood have been shown to improve mood and energy levels. All green leafy vegetables such as spinach and chard are excellent sources of B complex, while broccoli and peppers are rich in folate.

1. Process the broccoli, spinach, and chard through an electronic juicer according to the manufacturer's directions.

2. Add the bell pepper.

3. Stir the juice to combine the ingredients. Serve alone or over ice.

PER SERVING: Calories: 109 | Fat: 1g | Protein: 7.6g | Sodium: 364mg | Carbohydrates: 21g | Sugar: 8g

CHAPTER 12

Cold Soups

If you're a soup fan, it's not much of a leap to discover that the juicing lifestyle lends itself to a host of delicious variations. You can easily vary your juicing and raw foods routine through the addition of a variety of cold soups made with fresh fruits and vegetables. Chilled soups are ideal for hot weather dining, low in calories, and offer wonderful opportunities for experiment and adaptation. Leftover pulp from your fresh juices can be added to your soups as well, in order to derive every bit of goodness and additional dietary fiber. Even if you're not a cook, cold soups are as simple as it gets when it comes to culinary skills. From the garden or produce market to the table involves only a few ingredients, the right equipment, and a bit of imagination to master. So whether you like your soup cool and fruity, chunky or creamy, these healthy and delightful selections are sure to win the approval of family and friends.

Stocking Up

Many of the following recipes call for chicken stock or dairy products; vegans can easily substitute their favorite vegetable stocks as well as soy, almond, or rice milk products in those instances where yogurt or milk is called for in a recipe.

As someone once wrote: "Cooking is like love; it should be entered into fearlessly, or not at all." So begin with these healthy, nutritious, and delectable recipes and go on to come up with some classics of your own.

Soup's On!

Chilled Fennel Soup

Very French and so very good, this is an excellent choice for a summer lunch.

INGREDIENTS | SERVES 2

1 onion, peeled and chopped

1½ pounds fennel bulb, trimmed

2 tablespoons butter

5 cups vegetable or chicken stock

2 tablespoons chopped fresh chervil

1. Sauté the onion and fennel in the butter until translucent, about 3–5 minutes.

2. Cover with the stock; simmer 10 minutes or until tender.

3. Transfer the mixture to a blender and purée until smooth.

4. Chill and garnish with fresh chervil before serving.

PER SERVING: Calories: 126 | Fat: 0.7g | Protein: 6g | Sodium: 176mg | Carbohydrates: 29g | Sugar: 2g

Raw Versus Simmered?

If you prefer, juice the fennel and onion in this recipe, rather than simmering it in vegetable stock. Reserve the juice and pulp. Reduce the stock to 3 cups and process in a blender before chilling.

Melon Soup

Delish! The hint of chile and lime gives this recipe a Southwest flavor.

INGREDIENTS | SERVES 2

1 honeydew melon, peeled and seeded

2 tablespoons lime juice

2 teaspoons chili powder

1 cup low-fat plain yogurt

¼ cup fresh mint

1. Combine the ingredients in any order in the work bowl of a food processor or blender.

2. Purée until smooth.

3. Chill 1 hour or more. Whisk before serving and garnish with additional mint leaves as desired.

PER SERVING: Calories: 274 | Fat: 3g | Protein: 10g | Sodium: 204mg | Carbohydrates: 57g | Sugar: 49g

Watermelon Gazpacho

Another cold soup superstar, this unusual combination of watermelon with more traditional gazpacho ingredients adds a note of sweetness that makes it different from the rest!

INGREDIENTS | SERVES 4

½ pound tomatoes
4 cups watermelon chunks
1 medium cucumber
½ cup mint leaves
¼ cup olive oil
¼ cup crumbled feta cheese (optional)

1. Combine the ingredients in any order in the work bowl of a food processor or blender.

2. Pulse on and off just until blended and chunky.

3. Chill 1 hour or more. Garnish with crumbled feta cheese if desired.

PER SERVING: Calories: 195 | Fat: 14g | Protein: 2.5g | Sodium: 17mg | Carbohydrates: 18g | Sugar: 12g

Chilled Avocado Soup

Rich and delicious, this soup should be used the day it is made, otherwise the avocados may discolor a bit in the refrigerator.

INGREDIENTS | SERVES 6

3 medium avocados, peeled and pitted
½ cup white wine
¾ cup chicken stock
1 cup plain low-fat yogurt
1 cup sour cream
Generous dash of hot sauce
Fresh herbs for garnish (optional)

1. Combine the ingredients in the work bowl of a food processor or blender until smooth.

2. Chill 1 hour or more and garnish with fresh herbs as desired.

PER SERVING: Calories: 287 | Fat: 23g | Protein: 6g | Sodium: 110mg | Carbohydrates: 14g | Sugar: 5.5g

Chilled Cucumber Soup

Taste to "die for"? No way! This has a flavor you'll live for!

INGREDIENTS | SERVES 4

2 large cucumbers, sliced

2 scallions, trimmed and coarsely chopped

1 garlic clove, peeled

1 cup plain low-fat yogurt

4 tablespoons fresh dill

1 teaspoon salt

½ teaspoon ground black pepper

1. Combine the ingredients in the work bowl of a food processor or blender until smooth.

2. Chill 1 hour or more and garnish with additional dill as desired.

PER SERVING: Calories: 47 | Fat: 1g | Protein: 3.6g | Sodium: 634mg | Carbohydrates: 6.4g | Sugar: 5.3g

Greek Yogurt

For a richer taste that's lower in calories, substitute Greek yogurt for the low-fat yogurt called for in a recipe.

Cream of Mango Soup

The magical health benefits of mango matched with berries and citrus in an incredibly good tropical treat!

INGREDIENTS | SERVES 4

3 tablespoons dark rum

⅓ cup sugar

Juice and grated zest of 1 large lemon

1 large mango, peeled, pitted, and cut into chunks

4 cups half-and-half

Fresh berries, for garnish

1. Combine the ingredients in the work bowl of a food processor or blender and process until smooth.

2. Chill for 1 hour or more and garnish with berries as desired.

PER SERVING: Calories: 441 | Fat: 28g | Protein: 7.5g | Sodium: 100mg | Carbohydrates: 37g | Sugar: 25g

Soy Milk Facts

Studies indicate that soy milk increases estrogen production and may be helpful in balancing out menopausal symptoms. Soy milk can be substituted for the half-and-half in this recipe.

Cold Strawberry Soup

Buttermilk, like yogurt, is more easily digestible than whole milk and contains probiotics that promote healthy digestion.

INGREDIENTS | SERVES 4

1 pint strawberries, washed and hulled

2 cups buttermilk

⅓ cup raw honey

⅓ cup plain low-fat yogurt

4 tablespoons kirsch or other strawberry-flavored liqueur

1. Combine the ingredients in the work bowl of a food processor or blender and process until smooth.

2. Chill for 1 hour or more and garnish with additional strawberries as desired.

PER SERVING: Calories: 193 | Fat: 2.7g | Protein: 5.8g | Sodium: 151mg | Carbohydrates: 37g | Sugar: 35g

Oh, Honey!

Raw honey is nature's own multivitamin. Vitamins such as B_1, B_2, B_3, B_5, B_6, and even antioxidant-rich vitamin C are found in raw honey. It also contains minerals like magnesium, potassium, calcium, sodium, chlorine, sulphur, and phosphate.

Easy Gazpacho

This Southwestern classic actually originated in the Andalusian region of Spain.

INGREDIENTS | SERVES 6

1 bunch scallions, trimmed

3 garlic cloves, peeled

2 large green bell peppers, seeded and cut into chunks

2 medium cucumbers, sliced

3 large tomatoes

4 cups fresh tomato juice

¼ cup extra-virgin olive oil

2 tablespoons balsamic vinegar

1 teaspoon salt

½ teaspoon ground black pepper

1 tablespoon hot sauce

1. Process the vegetables in the work bowl of a food processor just until chunky.

2. Add the tomato juice and combine.

3. Add the olive oil, vinegar, and seasonings.

4. Chill for 1 hour or more.and serve with fresh, whole-grain bread.

PER SERVING: Calories: 157 | Fat: 9.4g | Protein: 3.3g | Sodium: 481mg | Carbohydrates: 18g | Sugar: 12g

Green Summer Soup

This cool soup is excellent topped with a sprinkling of grated Asiago cheese.

INGREDIENTS | SERVES 6

4 cups chicken or vegetable stock
1½ cups chopped green beans
½ cup chopped zucchini
½ cup chopped romaine lettuce
½ cup fresh peas
¾ cup chopped celery
½ cup chopped scallions
¼ cup chopped fresh basil
¼ cup chopped fresh parsley
1 teaspoon salt
½ teaspoon ground black pepper

1. Combine all ingredients in a large bowl or soup tureen.

2. Chill thoroughly or overnight before serving to allow flavors to blend.

PER SERVING: Calories: 92 | Fat: 3g | Protein: 5g | Sodium: 403mg | Carbohydrates: 13g | Sugar: 2.5g

Curried Zucchini Soup

Ayurvedic medicine touts the health benefits of curry powder, which is believed to be instrumental in curing a variety of ills.

INGREDIENTS | SERVES 6

2 cups chicken or vegetable stock

6 medium zucchini, ends removed, cut into 2-inch chunks

1 medium onion, coarsely chopped

1 tablespoon curry powder

¾ cup light cream

1. Place the ingredients in the work bowl of a food processor or blender and purée until smooth.

2. Chill for 1 hour or more and serve.

PER SERVING: Calories: 135 | Fat: 7.8g | Protein: 5g | Sodium: 178mg | Carbohydrates: 13g | Sugar: 5.7g

Curry

Studies suggest that curry can be instrumental as an anti-inflammatory and that it may aid or even prevent the advent of Alzheimer's disease.

Kiwi Soup

*Kiwis were originally called Chinese gooseberries until
New Zealand officially named them after their national bird.*

INGREDIENTS | SERVES 4

10 kiwis, peeled
1 cup apple juice
1 cup vanilla low-fat yogurt
2 tablespoons confectioners' sugar

A Matter of Choice

Confectioners' sugar contains cornstarch, which acts as a binding agent and helps to maintain the creamy texture of this soup. Use honey if you prefer, but whisk the soup to blend before serving.

1. Place all ingredients in the work bowl of a food processor or blender and purée until smooth.

2. Chill for 1 hour or more before serving.

PER SERVING: Calories: 211 | Fat: 1.6g | Protein: 4.9g | Sodium: 52mg | Carbohydrates: 47g | Sugar: 18g

Mixed Berry Soup

Use whatever berry mix you have available; sweet cherries are a nice addition, too!

INGREDIENTS | SERVES 4

3 cups mixed berries (raspberries, strawberries, blueberries, or blackberries)

1 cup vanilla low-fat yogurt

1 cup fresh orange juice

¼ cup zinfandel wine

2 tablespoons confectioners' sugar

1 teaspoon orange zest

1. Combine the ingredients in the work bowl of a food processor or blender and purée until smooth.

2. Chill for at least 2 hours and serve with a garnish of additional berries and orange zest.

PER SERVING: Calories: 155 | Fat: 1.5g | Protein: 4.5g | Sodium: 42mg | Carbohydrates: 30g | Sugar: 21g

Mango Chipotle Soup

The smoky flavor of powdered or canned chipotle peppers is a perfect complement to the fruit in this vegan offering.

INGREDIENTS | SERVES 4

2 mangoes, peeled and seeded

4 Mexican limes, peeled

1 teaspoon chipotle powder or 1 canned chipotle pepper

2 cups vegetable broth

1. Process the ingredients in the work bowl of a food processor or blender until smooth and creamy.

2. Chill at least 1 hour before serving and adjust the seasoning to taste.

PER SERVING: Calories: 87 | Fat: 0.4g | Protein: 1g | Sodium: 34mg | Carbohydrates: 24g | Sugar: 16g

Raw Corn Chowder

While most of us don't indulge in raw corn very often, there's nothing like it, fresh off the cob.

INGREDIENTS | SERVES 2

2 ears sweet yellow corn or white corn

2 cups almond milk

Raw Corn?

Raw corn can be difficult to digest for some, but it does contain vitamin C, magnesium, and phosphorus, which are not found in cooked corn.

1. Cut the corn from the cob.

2. Combine the corn with the almond milk in the work bowl of a blender. Process until smooth.

3. Chill at least 1 hour before serving.

PER SERVING: Calories: 202 | Fat: 4.9g | Protein: 11g | Sodium: 91mg | Carbohydrates: 33g | Sugar: 5.7g

Curried Carrot Soup

Curry and carrot make a great combination of sweetness and spice.

INGREDIENTS | SERVES 2

Fresh juice from 1 pound carrots

2 cups chicken or vegetable broth

2 tablespoons grated ginger

2 teaspoons curry powder

1 cup low-fat plain yogurt

¼ cup fresh orange juice

1. Combine the ingredients in a blender and process until smooth.

2. Chill at least 1 hour before serving.

PER SERVING: Calories: 452 | Fat: 5.8g | Protein: 19g | Sodium: 398mg | Carbohydrates: 77g | Sugar: 41g

CHAPTER 13

Smoothies and Frozen Treats

When it comes to the wide, wonderful world of smoothies and frozen treats you can let your imagination run wild. There's little that's more tempting than these healthy (and sometimes hearty) concoctions: sweet and creamy or icy and refreshing. You can add nuts for additional protein and fats, yogurt or other dairy products, or even soy, coconut, or rice milk to turn your fresh fruits and veggies into a taste sensation.

Healthy Treats

It's important to remember that not all smoothies and frozen treats are created equal. Some are loaded with sugars and fats; some can take your best intentions for better dietary practice down a path where they do more harm than good. That's not to say that you can't indulge yourself from time to time, just that, like everything else in life, balance is key. Watch your fats and calories; don't overload on unnecessary refined sugars when raw honey or alternative sweeteners will do just as well, and be aware that some combinations, for all their appeal, can be hard on the digestive system.

Yet smoothies and frozen concoctions remain a wonderful way to vary your juicing practice by adding new flavors, colors, and textures to your diet. They are a wonderful way to stay healthy and keep up your consumption of fresh fruits and vegetables to maintain optimum nutrition, particularly when a busy lifestyle makes a balanced breakfast or a leisurely, satisfying lunch impossible.

There are recipes here to satisfy everyone from the most passionate vegan to the wide-eyed kid who wants his ice cream. So whatever your dietary preferences, or your family's needs, these fresh, wholesome, and satisfying selections surely hold something for everyone.

Satisfying Smoothies and Cool Concoctions

Green Energy Smoothie

This good-for-you smoothie is essential for that midafternoon slump or any time you need a lift.

INGREDIENTS | YIELDS 1½ CUPS

½ cup baby spinach
1 apple, cored
1 banana, peeled
1 cup low-fat plain yogurt
6 strawberries, stems removed
½ orange, peeled

1. Place all the ingredients in a blender and process until smooth.

2. Serve immediately.

PER SERVING: Calories: 393 | Fat: 4.7g | Protein: 16g | Sodium: 185mg | Fiber: 8.5g | Carbohydrates: 78g | Sugar: 57g

Why Yogurt?

Everyone knows your body needs to have a healthy amount of "good" bacteria in the digestive tract, and many yogurts are made using active, good bacteria. Like the fruits and veggies in many smoothies, it contains enzymes that aid digestion and help fight off disease. You'll often see the word *probiotic* associated with yogurts. Probiotic literally means "for life," and refers to living organisms that result in health benefits when eaten in adequate amounts.

Apple Berry Smoothie

Use any berries you have on hand or a combination of the three listed below.

INGREDIENTS | YIELDS 1½ CUPS

1 cup plain low-fat yogurt

1 cup strawberries, blueberries, or raspberries

¾ cup skim milk

¾ cup fresh apple juice

Combine all the ingredients in a blender and process until smooth.

PER SERVING: Calories: 362 | Fat: 6.2g | Protein: 20g | Sodium: 260mg | Fiber: 3.2g | Carbohydrates: 58g | Sugar: 51g

Strawberry Banana Smoothie

If your blender doesn't handle ice well, crush it first and freeze the fruit before blending.

INGREDIENTS | YIELDS 1½ CUPS

1 banana, peeled

1 cup strawberries, stems removed

2 teaspoons raw honey

½ cup skim milk

1 teaspoon vanilla extract

1 cup ice

1. Combine all the ingredients in a blender and purée until smooth.

2. Serve immediately.

PER SERVING: Calories: 242 | Fat: 2g | Protein: 6.2g | Sodium: 57mg | Fiber: 5.5g | Carbohydrates: 52g | Sugar: 37g

Berry Blender Special

Super berries together again in a dairy-based smoothie that holds the line on calories.

INGREDIENTS | YIELDS 1½ CUPS

½ cup blackberries

1 cup strawberries, stems removed

½ cup raspberries

1 cup skim milk

1 cup ice

1. Combine all the ingredients in a blender and purée until smooth.

2. Serve immediately.

PER SERVING: Calories: 211 | Fat: 3.5g | Protein: 11g | Sodium: 110mg | Fiber: 10g | Carbohydrates: 37g | Sugar: 25g

Honeydew Almond Smoothie

Almond milk doesn't contribute to high cholesterol and contains potassium for heart health. So drink up!

INGREDIENTS | YIELDS 1½ CUPS

2 cups honeydew melon chunks

1 cup almond milk

1 cup ice

1. Combine all the ingredients in a blender and purée until smooth.

2. Serve immediately.

PER SERVING: Calories: 202 | Fat: 4.4g | Protein: 8.8g | Sodium: 146mg | Fiber: 3.6g | Carbohydrates: 34g | Sugar: 28g

Cherry Almond Smoothie

*Another great smoothie featuring almond milk, it perfectly complements
the flavor of fresh sweet cherries.*

INGREDIENTS | YIELDS 1½ CUPS

1½ cups frozen pitted cherries

1¼ cups almond milk

1 teaspoon almond extract

2 teaspoons raw honey

1 cup ice

1. Combine all the ingredients in a blender and purée until smooth.

2. Serve immediately.

PER SERVING: Calories: 288 | Fat: 5.4g | Protein: 11g | Sodium: 106mg | Fiber: 6g | Carbohydrates: 53g | Sugar: 42g

Spa Smoothie

Healthy and refreshing, this is as good as a trip to the day spa.

INGREDIENTS | YIELDS 1½ CUPS

2 medium cucumbers, peeled and cut into chunks

Juice of 1 lime

½ cup filtered water

1 cup ice

3 teaspoons raw honey

1 cup ice

1. Combine the ingredients in a blender and purée until smooth.

2. Serve immediately.

PER SERVING: Calories: 174 | Fat: 0.7g | Protein: 4.4g | Sodium: 14mg | Fiber: 5g | Carbohydrates: 46g | Sugar: 28g

Hot Date Smoothie

While sweet and succulent dates do contain sugars, they also supply necessary fiber.
Dates are also an excellent source of vitamin A, iron, and other minerals.

INGREDIENTS | YIELDS 1½ CUPS

2 bananas, peeled and cut into chunks
¾ cup chopped pitted dates
Juice of 1 lime
1½ cups soy milk

1. Combine all the ingredients in a blender and purée until smooth.

2. Serve immediately.

PER SERVING: Calories: 726 | Fat: 7.4g | Protein: 16g | Sodium: 133mg | Fiber: 20g | Carbohydrates: 167g | Sugar: 116g

Ginger Peachy Smoothie

Vanilla yogurt complements this healthy blend. You can peel the peaches if you prefer.

INGREDIENTS | YIELDS 1½ CUPS

3 large yellow or white peaches, pitted
1 (¼-inch) piece fresh ginger
1 cup low-fat vanilla yogurt
½ cup ice

1. Combine all the ingredients in a blender and purée until smooth.

2. Serve immediately.

PER SERVING: Calories: 431 | Fat: 4.6g | Protein: 17g | Sodium: 163mg | Fiber: 8.5g | Carbohydrates: 87g | Sugar: 78g

Smoothie History

Health food stores on the West Coast of the United States began selling puréed fruit drinks in the 1930s, based on recipes that originated in Brazil. They gained increased popularity during the late '60s and early '70s when people showed renewed interest in vegetarianism.

PB & J Smoothie

If you like peanut butter and jelly, this smoothie is for you!

INGREDIENTS | YIELDS 1½ CUPS

2 cups Concord grapes
2 tablespoons smooth peanut butter
1½ cups almond milk
1 cup ice

1. Combine all the ingredients in a blender and purée until smooth.

2. Serve immediately.

PER SERVING: Calories: 518 | Fat: 22g | Protein: 20g | Sodium: 281mg | Fiber: 6g | Carbohydrates: 66g | Sugar: 51g

Kiwi-Strawberry Blend

This one has no added yogurt or milk, just the goodness of fresh fruit.

INGREDIENTS | YIELDS 1 CUP

1 cup strawberries, stems removed
2 kiwis, peeled
2 tablespoons raw honey
2 cups ice

1. Combine all the ingredients in a blender and purée until smooth.

2. Serve immediately.

PER SERVING: Calories: 267 | Fat: 1g | Protein: 2.5g | Sodium: 10mg | Fiber: 8g | Carbohydrates: 68g | Sugar: 41g

Blueberry-Banana Smoothie

Mmm-mm, good! This is one of the best breakfast smoothies of all time.

INGREDIENTS | YIELDS 1½ CUPS

1 banana, peeled
1 cup blueberries
½ cup coconut milk
2 tablespoons raw honey
Juice of 1 small lime
1 cup ice

1. Combine all the ingredients in a blender and purée until smooth.

2. Serve immediately.

PER SERVING: Calories: 420 | Fat: 15g | Protein: 5g | Sodium: 20mg | Fiber: 8.5g | Carbohydrates: 90g | Sugar: 65g

Watermelon Freeze

Popsicle good and so few calories, this is an excellent choices for those watching their weight.

INGREDIENTS | YIELDS 1½ CUPS

3 cups frozen watermelon chunks
1 cup cubed fresh seeded watermelon
Juice of 1 lime
¼ cup sugar
1 cup water

1. Combine all the ingredients in a blender and purée until smooth.

2. Serve immediately.

PER SERVING: Calories: 397 | Fat: 1g | Protein: 4g | Sodium: 8mg | Fiber: 4g | Carbohydrates: 103g | Sugar: 89g

Freeze Your Fruit

Instead of using ice in smoothie or slush recipes, try prefreezing your fruit for more concentrated flavor.

Black Raspberry-Vanilla Smoothie

Black raspberries can be hard to find,
but blending blackberries and red raspberries together is a great substitute.

INGREDIENTS | YIELDS 1½ CUPS

2 cups blackberries
½ cup raspberries
1 cup low-fat vanilla yogurt
2 tablespoons raw honey

1. Combine all the ingredients in a blender and purée until smooth.

2. Serve immediately.

PER SERVING: Calories: 492 | Fat: 5g | Protein: 17g | Sodium: 166mg | Fiber: 19g | Carbohydrates: 103g | Sugar: 85g

Mango-Acai Smoothie

Acai berry purée is available in the frozen section of health and specialty food shops.
The fruit of the acai palm, these berries are touted as a superfood due to their many
health benefits for weight loss, anti-aging, and antioxidant properties.

INGREDIENTS | YIELDS 1½ CUPS

2 (4-ounce) packages frozen acai berry purée
1 cup chopped mango
1 orange, peeled and seeded
2 cups ice

1. Combine all the ingredients in a blender and purée until smooth.

2. Serve immediately.

PER SERVING: Calories: 232 | Fat: 1g | Protein: 3g | Sodium: 4.4mg | Fiber: 8g | Carbohydrates: 59g | Sugar: 47g

Pumpkin Pie Smoothie

This recipe uses silken tofu for added richness and nutrition.

INGREDIENTS | YIELDS 1½ CUPS

½ cup puréed fresh pumpkin
½ cup silken tofu
¼ cup dark brown sugar
1 cup skim milk
1 teaspoon pumpkin pie spice

1. Combine all the ingredients in a blender and purée until smooth.

2. Serve immediately.

PER SERVING: Calories: 388 | Fat: 5.4g | Protein: 14g | Sodium: 128mg | Fiber: 1g | Carbohydrates: 73g | Sugar: 68g

Cucumber Jalapeño Slush

Always trim and seed jalapeños before adding to your recipes, using plastic gloves if possible, as the juice and seeds can irritate your skin.

INGREDIENTS | YIELDS 1½ CUPS

2 cucumbers, peeled and sliced
3 kales leaves, chopped
1 cup fresh tomato juice
Juice of ½ lemon
1 fresh jalapeño pepper, seeded
1 cup ice

1. Combine all the ingredients in a blender and purée until smooth.

2. Serve immediately.

PER SERVING: Calories: 177 | Fat: 1.4g | Protein: 8.4g | Sodium: 65mg | Fiber: 6.5g | Carbohydrates: 42g | Sugar: 19g

Lemon–Poppy Seed Smoothie

*Poppy seeds contain iron, phosphorus, and fiber,
and are thought to aid in the prevention of kidney stones.*

INGREDIENTS | YIELDS 1½ CUPS

2 teaspoons poppy seeds

Juice and zest of 1 lemon

1 cup vanilla low-fat yogurt

2 tablespoons raw honey

½ cup low-fat milk

½ cup ice

1. Combine all the ingredients in a blender and purée until smooth.

2. Serve immediately.

PER SERVING: Calories: 359 | Fat: 5g | Protein: 17g | Sodium: 218mg | Fiber: 2.8g | Carbohydrates: 81g | Sugar: 76g

Ice Cream in a Minute

There's nothing like homemade ice cream, and this recipe is so easy, you'll never be without it!

**INGREDIENTS | YIELDS 2 CUPS
(4 SERVINGS)**

2 cups frozen berries

2 cups low-fat plain Greek yogurt

2 tablespoons raw honey

Combine all the ingredients in a blender and enjoy! Mixture can be refrozen in a covered container.

PER SERVING: Calories: 149 | Fat: 4g | Protein: 8g | Sodium: 57mg | Fiber: 2g | Carbohydrates: 25g | Sugar: 21g

Apple-Spinach Smoothie

Healthy and delicious, this gets an extra nutritional punch with the addition of wheat germ.

INGREDIENTS | YIELDS 1½ CUPS

2 cups spinach

1 apple, cored and cut into chunks

½ cup silken tofu

1 tablespoon wheat germ

½ cup soy milk

½ cup fresh orange juice

1 cup ice

Combine all the ingredients in a blender and process until smooth. Enjoy!

PER SERVING: Calories: 274 | Fat: 6g | Protein: 13g | Sodium: 97mg | Fiber: 5g | Carbohydrates: 44g | Sugar: 28g

Veggie Ice

Tasty and refreshing, this recipe provides a little light nourishment to keep you fit and fabulous!

INGREDIENTS | YIELDS 1½ CUPS

1¼ cups fresh tomato juice

¼ cup fresh carrot juice

1 stalk celery, with leaves

¼ cup spinach

¼ cup parsley

1 cup ice

1. Combine all the ingredients in a blender and process until smooth.

2. Serve immediately.

PER SERVING: Calories: 88 | Fat: 0.4g | Protein: 3.8g | Sodium: 93mg | Fiber: 3g | Carbohydrates: 20g | Sugar: 14g

Pomegranate Freeze

Juice the pomegranates and beets separately for this recipe.

INGREDIENTS | YIELDS 1½ CUPS

¾ cup fresh beet juice

¾ cup fresh pomegranate juice

1 cup blueberries

2 tablespoons raw honey

1 cup ice

Combine all the ingredients in a blender and process until smooth.

PER SERVING: Calories: 325 | Fat: 0.8g | Protein: 3g | Sodium: 90mg | Fiber: 3g | Carbohydrates: 87g | Sugar: 72g

Whole Blueberries

Some sources say that the highest concentration of blueberry nutrients are in the skin and the pulp, so use whole berries rather than juice for this recipe.

Apricot Almond Delight

If you have a masticating or auger-style juicer, you can make your own almond butter.

INGREDIENTS | YIELDS 2½ CUPS (2 SERVINGS)

1½ cups fresh apricot nectar

1 cup vanilla low-fat yogurt

2 tablespoons almond butter

1 tablespoon raw honey

1 cup ice

Combine all the ingredients in a blender and process until smooth.

PER SERVING: Calories: 306 | Fat: 5g | Protein: 8g | Sodium: 88mg | Fiber: 1.8g | Carbohydrates: 59g | Sugar: 56g

Creamsicle Shake

Childhood flavor with grown-up nutrition, there's no comparison between this and the stuff that comes from your grocer's freezer.

**INGREDIENTS | YIELDS 2½ CUPS
(2 SERVINGS)**

1½ cups fresh orange juice
1 tangerine, peeled and seeded
1 cup vanilla ice cream
1 cup ice

Combine all the ingredients in a blender and process until smooth.

PER SERVING: Calories: 261 | Fat: 8g | Protein: 4g | Sodium: 60mg | Fiber: 1.8g | Carbohydrates: 43g | Sugar: 36g

Gelato Versus Ice Cream

The Italian version of ice cream, gelato, is, despite its rich, egg-based custard base, actually lower in fat than other ice creams. Try replacing the ice cream in the recipe with gelato for a richer shake.

Jalapeño Mint Slush

Cooling mint and hot pepper combine in this awesome cooler. For a Greek variation of this smoothie, add ½ cucumber and a clove of garlic and omit the jalapeño.

**INGREDIENTS | YIELDS 2½ CUPS
(2 SERVINGS)**

½ cup fresh mint
1 jalapeño, seeded
2½ tablespoons raw honey
2 cups plain low-fat yogurt
2 cups ice

Combine all the ingredients in a blender and process until smooth.

PER SERVING: Calories: 242 | Fat: 7g | Protein: 9g | Sodium: 120mg | Fiber: 1.7g | Carbohydrates: 35g | Sugar: 33g

Green Tea Smoothie

Green tea has been shown to have beneficial effects on weight loss and metabolism.

**INGREDIENTS | YIELDS 2½ CUPS
(2 SERVINGS)**

1 frozen banana, chopped

6 frozen strawberries

1 kiwi, peeled

2½ tablespoons raw honey

2 cups green tea

½ cup ice

Combine all the ingredients in a blender and process until smooth.

PER SERVING: Calories: 169 | Fat: 0.3g | Protein: 1.2g | Sodium: 11mg | Fiber: 3.5g | Carbohydrates: 44g | Sugar: 30g

Chocolate Banana Shake

Not just for chocoholics anymore, dark chocolate has been shown to have beneficial effects on mood and blood pressure.

INGREDIENTS | YIELDS 2 CUPS

1 banana, peeled

1 cup dark chocolate ice cream

½ cup ice

Dash of plain chili powder

Combine all the ingredients in a blender and process until smooth.

PER SERVING: Calories: 187 | Fat: 7g | Protein: 3g | Sodium: 50mg | Fiber: 2g | Carbohydrates: 30g | Sugar: 22g

The Chile Chocolate Secret

Long a Mexican and Southwestern tradition, the addition of chili powder to chocolate adds a subtle depth and intensifies the chocolate flavor. Once you've tried it, there's no going back!

Chocolate Raspberry Shake

Even though this makes a generous portion, you'll discover it's too good to share!

INGREDIENTS | YIELDS 1½ CUPS

1 cup chocolate ice cream

1 cup frozen raspberries

¾ cup ice

¾ cup skim milk

Combine all the ingredients in a blender and process until smooth.

PER SERVING: Calories: 619 | Fat: 16g | Protein: 12g | Sodium: 183mg | Fiber: 12g | Carbohydrates: 111g | Sugar: 97g

Caramel Apple Smoothie

This smoothie version of caramel apples is almost better than the ones on a stick!

INGREDIENTS | YIELDS 1½ CUPS

1 apple, cored

1 cup caramel or praline ice cream

2 tablespoons peanut butter

¾ cup ice

Combine all the ingredients in a blender and process until smooth.

PER SERVING: Calories: 564 | Fat: 32g | Protein: 13g | Sodium: 263mg | Fiber: 5g | Carbohydrates: 60g | Sugar: 49g

Cherry Pomegranate Smoothie

Juice the pomegranate separately for this recipe, or use purchased fresh pomegranate juice.

INGREDIENTS | YIELDS 1½ CUPS

1 cup frozen pitted cherries

1 cup fresh pomegranate juice

1 cup plain or vanilla low-fat yogurt

1 tablespoon raw honey

2 cups ice

Combine all the ingredients in a blender and process until smooth.

PER SERVING: Calories: 428 | Fat: 8g | Protein: 10g | Sodium: 123mg | Fiber: 3.5g | Carbohydrates: 82g | Sugar: 69g

CHAPTER 14

Pulp with a Purpose

Sooner or later, every avid juicer has a conversation with themselves about pulp. After all, if you juice regularly, it has to occur to you that you may be throwing away a lot of useful leftovers. Juicers tend to fall into two groups when it comes to the subject of repurposing pulp. The first sees little value in finding other uses for your fruit and vegetable pulp, while the second, and perhaps thriftier crowd, tends to go with the "waste not, want not" school of household economy.

Which Pulp to Use

Two things are going to affect your decision to use the pulp from your juicer for other culinary purposes. The first is just how effective your juicer is at making juice. If the pulp it leaves behind is very fibrous and dry, it probably doesn't look too appetizing and probably isn't going to add a lot to other recipes except fiber. But if you own a centrifugal juicer, there's a lot more moisture and useable foodstuffs left behind.

But juice pulp can add a lot of healthy ingredients to your recipes. It can be used to thicken sauces and be added to pasta fillings, poultry stuffings, jams, and just about anything else you might dream up.

Choose what you use wisely, though. Be aware that some fruits and veggies are thought to contain even more nutrient value than the juice itself—blueberries and grapes, for example. Others, such as pomegranate or mango seeds, don't make such an appealing addition to your morning scones. If you intend to use your pulp, refrigerate it immediately and use it within twenty-four hours. If you freeze it, be aware that some veggies and fruits are more freezer friendly, while others, those with a higher moisture content, like cucumbers, for example, may thaw into an unappealing green slime.

Ten More Uses for Juicing Pulp: Get Creative!

While there's no real recipe attached to any of the following suggestions, each is a fabulous and thrifty use for repurposing your juicing pulp:

- Stir vegetable pulp into soups and stews to thicken broth and pump up the flavor.
- Add ½ cup pulp to your favorite muffin or scone recipe; fruit for sweet and vegetable for savory.
- Stir a couple of cups of vegetable pulp into cooked couscous, quinoa, or kasha for an instant tabouli-type salad.
- Add beet, spinach, or other vegetable pulp to basic pasta dough recipes for colorful and healthy homemade pasta.
- Stir some carrot or squash pulp into your child's macaroni and cheese for extra nutrition.

- Add 1 cup of vegetable pulp to poultry stuffing for a lighter, more nutritious alternative.
- Adding vegetable pulp to your dog's food helps maintain his digestive tracts.
- Turn leftover pulp into garden soil as a natural compost and fertilizer.
- Dried pulps can be mixed with bird seed and chicken feed.
- Some pulps, such as cucumber, avocado, citrus, aloe, and grape, make great facials. Just add water and a bit of olive oil to make a paste, lie back, and relax!

As always, use your head and feel free to experiment. In no time at all, you can turn your pulp into a series of culinary triumphs.

Recipes That Pulp It Up

Pumpkin Pulp Pasta Sauce

This is an adaptation of a traditional northern Italian pasta sauce.
Made with cream, pumpkin, and fresh sage, it's out of this world.

INGREDIENTS | SERVES 4

1 cup fresh pumpkin pulp
2 cups chicken or vegetable broth
1 cup heavy cream
1 teaspoon nutmeg
¼ cup chopped fresh sage

1. Place the pulp and the broth in a saucepan and simmer over medium heat until slightly thickened.

2. Add the cream and the nutmeg. Blend and simmer without allowing the sauce to boil until reduced by a third, about 10 minutes.

3. Stir in the fresh sage. Serve over hot cooked pasta with fresh ground pepper.

Chunky Tomato Pasta Sauce

Fresh pulp adds texture and flavor to an otherwise bland jarred sauce.

INGREDIENTS | SERVES 4

1 (16-ounce) jar pasta sauce
1 cup plain tomato pulp or mixed vegetable pulp
¼ cup chopped fresh basil
½ cup green olives

1. Place the sauce and the pulp in a saucepan and simmer over medium heat until slightly thickened, about 10 minutes.

2. Add the basil and the olives and heat through, about 3 minutes.

3. Serve over hot cooked pasta with fresh ground pepper and Romano cheese.

Salsa Guacamole

Salsa lends itself to a host of great additions—consider adding cilantro, black beans, or chopped tomatillos to liven up your guacamole.

INGREDIENTS | SERVES 6

3 large avocados, peeled, seeded, and mashed

4 green onions, chopped

Juice of 1 lime

1½ cups plain tomato pulp

Combine all the ingredients in a large bowl. Chill before serving.

Thai Pesto

This makes an especially good sauce for fish or poultry.

INGREDIENTS | SERVES 8

1 cup chopped fresh mint

2 cloves garlic, minced

2 stalks lemongrass, chopped

Juice of 1 lime

3 cups chopped cilantro

¼ cup sesame oil

¼ cup citrus pulp of your choice

1. Process all the ingredients in the work bowl of a food processor or blender until smooth.

2. Store, covered, in the refrigerator for up to 2 weeks.

Chili Corn Salsa

Add a can of black beans to this fresh salsa for extra nutrition.

INGREDIENTS | SERVES 4

2 ears of fresh corn, kernels cut from the cob

1 red bell pepper, seeded and chopped

1 banana pepper, seeded and chopped

1 cup chopped red onion

½ cup carrot or tomato pulp

½ teaspoon chili powder

Combine ingredients in a large bowl and chill. Serve with chips or crackers.

Strawberry Leather

If you have a dehydrator, this is one of the best uses for fruit pulp. Try it with different types of fruit pulp.

INGREDIENTS | MAKES 24 STRIPS (12 SERVINGS)

2 cups strawberry pulp

4 tablespoons raw honey

1. In a large bowl, mix the strawberry pulp and honey together.

2. Spread mixture in a thin layer over 2 sheets of waxed paper.

3. Place each sheet in your dehydrator according to the manufacturer's directions.

4. Cut into strips and roll up. Store in plastic bags.

Purple Pancakes

Experts say the great nutrition in blueberries stays behind even after juicing. Use a pancake mix or make your own. Homemade Blueberry Syrup adds a great touch (see recipe in this chapter).

INGREDIENTS | MAKES 12 PANCAKES

2 cups blueberry pulp
2 cups prepared pancake batter
1 tablespoon vegetable oil

1. In a large bowl, mix the blueberry pulp and pancake batter together.

2. Heat the oil in a large griddle or skillet over medium-high heat.

3. Pour batter by ¼ cupfuls on the griddle. Cook until bubbles form on the surface, then turn and cook until lightly browned, about 3 minutes per side.

Blueberry Syrup

IHOP, eat your heart out. This homemade version of blueberry syrup is something you won't ever want to be without.

INGREDIENTS | MAKES 1 CUP

½ cup blueberry pulp
½ cup honey or maple syrup

Process pulp and honey or syrup in the work bowl of a food processor or blender to combine. Store in the refrigerator up to 1 month.

Carrot Pulp Cake

Don't confine yourself to just carrot pulp for this one. Use any combination of carrot, pineapple, zucchini, pumpkin, or other fruit. Even tomato pulp works!

INGREDIENTS | SERVES 8

3 cups self-rising flour
1½ cups dark brown sugar
¾ cup vegetable oil
4 eggs
2 cups carrot pulp
1 cup coconut
½ cup walnut pieces
2 teaspoons cinnamon

1. Preheat oven to 350°F. Grease and flour a 10-inch Bundt pan.

2. In a large bowl, blend the flour and the sugar thoroughly. Make a well in the center and add the oil and the eggs. Beat until smooth.

3. Stir in the carrot pulp, coconut, nuts, and cinnamon. Blend well.

4. Turn the batter into the prepared pan and bake for 1 hour, or until an inserted toothpick comes out clean.

Veggie Cream Cheese

Why pay for the high-priced cream cheese spread when you can make your own? Fruit, especially berry pulp, works well in this recipe, too.

INGREDIENTS | SERVES 6

8 ounces cream cheese, softened
1 cup mixed veggie pulp

In a small bowl, combine the softened cream cheese with the veggie pulp until well blended. Store in the refrigerator for up to 2 weeks.

Cruciferous Chow-Chow

Chow-chow is a mixed vegetable relish, traditionally eaten with beans or pork.
It's great on veggie burgers, too!

INGREDIENTS | MAKES 6 CUPS

3½ cups broccoli or cauliflower pulp
1 chopped red pepper
1 cup chopped onion
½ cup grated cabbage
1½ cups vinegar
¾ cup brown sugar
1 teaspoon turmeric
½ teaspoon ground cloves

1. Place all the ingredients in a large saucepan.

2. Heat to boiling and cook for 10 minutes.

3. Pour into clean glass or plastic containers and store in the refrigerator, for up to 2 months.

Veggie Fritters

These delicate, crisp fried pancakes will have your family begging for more!

INGREDIENTS | SERVES 6

1½ cups mixed vegetable pulp
½ cup flour
1 teaspoon baking powder
2 eggs
½ cup fresh grated Parmesan cheese
¼ cup vegetable oil

1. In a large bowl, combine the pulp, flour, baking powder, eggs, and cheese.

2. Heat ¼ cup vegetable oil in a large frying pan over medium-high heat.

3. Drop the vegetable mixture by spoonfuls in the hot oil.

4. When edges are brown and crisp, turn and fry on the other side until golden, about 3 minutes per side. Drain on paper towels and serve immediately.

Veggie Burgers

These pulp-enhanced burgers are hearty, healthy, and just plain good!
You can chop and mix all the ingredients in a food processor, too.

INGREDIENTS | SERVES 6

1½ cups mixed veggie pulp
2 tablespoons vegetable oil
1 onion, diced
1 clove garlic, minced
3 green onions, diced
½ teaspoon cumin
¾ cup diced fresh mushrooms
1 (15-ounce) can pinto beans, drained
2 tablespoons chopped fresh parsley
1 teaspoon salt
½ teaspoon ground black pepper

1. Combine all the ingredients in a large bowl and mix well.

2. Shape mixture into 6 patties.

3. Spray a large skillet with cooking spray and heat over medium heat. Fry patties until browned, about 8 minutes per side.

Southwestern Veggie Burgers

A Southwest version with a kick, this burger uses black beans.

INGREDIENTS | SERVES 6

1½ cups mixed bell pepper–based veggie pulp

2 tablespoons vegetable oil

1 onion, diced

1 clove garlic, minced

1 red pepper, diced

1 teaspoon cumin

1 egg

1 (15-ounce) can black beans, drained

2 tablespoons chopped fresh parsley

½ cup seasoned bread crumbs

1. Combine all the ingredients in a large bowl and mix well.

2. Shape mixture into 6 patties.

3. Spray a large skillet with cooking spray and heat over medium heat. Fry patties until browned, about 8 minutes per side.

Carrot-Lentil Burgers

This one uses lentils and carrot-based pulp for great flavor.

INGREDIENTS | SERVES 6

¼ cup finely chopped onion

½ cup carrot pulp

2 tablespoons olive oil

3 cups cooked lentils, mashed

2 tablespoons chopped, fresh parsley

¼ cup tomato pulp

¼ cup bread crumbs

1 teaspoon salt

1. Combine all the ingredients in a large bowl and mix well.

2. Shape mixture into 6 patties.

3. Spray a large skillet with cooking spray and heat over medium heat. Fry patties until browned, about 8 minutes per side.

Vegetable Stock

*Nothing could be easier! Vegetable pulp, salt, and water,
and you've got the base for wonderful homemade soups!*

INGREDIENTS | MAKES 4 CUPS

3 cups vegetable pulp

2 quarts water

2 teaspoons salt

1. Cover the pulp with the water in a large saucepan and cook over medium heat until the liquid is reduced by half, about 20 minutes.

2. Strain and discard the pulp. Season stock with salt.

3. Store in the refrigerator for up to 2 weeks or freeze for later use.

APPENDIX A

Glossary

Amino acid

A molecule that is the basic ingredient necessary to create a protein.

Anthocyanin

Any of various water-soluble pigments that impart to flowers and other plant parts colors ranging from violet and blue to most shades of red.

Antibacterial

Destroying or inhibiting the growth of bacteria

Anti-inflammatory

Preventing or reducing inflammation or swelling

Antioxidant

A molecule capable of inhibiting the oxidation of other molecules

Antiviral

Preventing or inhibiting the growth of viruses

Bioavailability

The degree to which a drug or other substance becomes available to the target tissue after administration.

Carminative

Any agent that induces the expulsion of gas from the stomach and intestines.

Carotene

An orange-yellow to red crystalline pigment, found in animal tissue and certain plants, such as carrots and squash

Chlorophyll

Any of a group of green pigments that are found in the chloroplasts of plants and in other photosynthetic organisms

Diuretic

A substance or drug that tends to increase the discharge of urine. Diuretics are used in the treatment of high blood pressure, edema, and other medical conditions.

Flavonoids

Any of a large group of water-soluble plant pigments, including the anthocyanins, that are beneficial to health.

Folate

A naturally occurring member of the B vitamin family important in DNA and red blood cell repair

Inulin

A zero-calorie, sweet inert carbohydrate

Phytonutrients or Phytochemicals

Compounds in plants (apart from vitamins, minerals, and macronutrients) that have a beneficial effect on the body.

Phytosterols
Cholesterol-like molecules found in plants. Plant sterols lower cholesterol levels in humans.

Resveratrol
A natural compound found in grapes, mulberries, peanuts, and other plants or food products, especially red wine, that may protect against cancer and cardiovascular disease by acting as an antioxidant and anti-inflammatory.

Soluble Fiber
A type of fiber that, when consumed, passes through the body and is excreted, rather than being absorbed into the bloodstream. This type of fiber is "soluble," or able to mix with water.

Sulforaphane
An anticarcinogenic found in cruciferous vegetables that is thought to function by stimulating the production of enzymes in the body that detoxify cancer-causing substances.

Xenoestrogen
A type of xenohormone that imitates estrogen

Online Resources

Great Websites for Juicing Enthusiasts

The following is a useful list of Internet resources for learning more about juicing, juice fasting, places to order juicers online, and general nutrition.

www.living-foods.com
Dedicated to the benefits of living and raw foods.

www.best-health-juicing.com
Information, recipes, true stories, and more.

www.juicingbook.com/recipes/mrsprout
Free online juicing book, lots of recipes, and general information from
"Mr. Sprout."

www.dole.com/DoleHTMLNutritionInstitute/
tabid/1169/Default.aspx
The Dole Nutrition Institute website, founded by Dole's CEO David Murdock, a lifelong advocate of healthy eating practices

www.thejuicenut.com
Site offers recipes, nutrition facts, and links to a host of online resources.

www.prolificliving.com
Smart habits for healthy and prolific living.

www.livestrong.com
A huge resource for healthy living, juice recipes, and nutritional information.

www.all-about-juicing.com
Advice and tips on juicing, and juice fasting.

Where to Research and Buy Juicers Online

www.squidoo.com/
top-10-best-rated-juicers-2012
Rates the top ten juicers for 2012 with buy links.

http://10rate.com/best-juicer-reviews
Another top ten ratings for juicers list, this one provides for every kind
of juicers in a wide variety of price ranges.

www.bestbuy.com
A very nice selection in a wide range of prices.

www.discountjuicers.com
Selling juicers online since 1998.

www.overstock.com
A quick search brought up seventy-five different juicers in a wide range
of prices.

Standard U.S./Metric Measurement Conversions

VOLUME CONVERSIONS

U.S. Volume Measure	Metric Equivalent
⅛ teaspoon	0.5 milliliter
¼ teaspoon	1 milliliter
½ teaspoon	2 milliliters
1 teaspoon	5 milliliters
½ tablespoon	7 milliliters
1 tablespoon (3 teaspoons)	15 milliliters
2 tablespoons (1 fluid ounce)	30 milliliters
¼ cup (4 tablespoons)	60 milliliters
⅓ cup	90 milliliters
½ cup (4 fluid ounces)	125 milliliters
⅔ cup	160 milliliters
¾ cup (6 fluid ounces)	180 milliliters
1 cup (16 tablespoons)	250 milliliters
1 pint (2 cups)	500 milliliters
1 quart (4 cups)	1 liter (about)

WEIGHT CONVERSIONS

U.S. Weight Measure	Metric Equivalent
½ ounce	15 grams
1 ounce	30 grams
2 ounces	60 grams
3 ounces	85 grams
¼ pound (4 ounces)	115 grams
½ pound (8 ounces)	225 grams
¾ pound (12 ounces)	340 grams
1 pound (16 ounces)	454 grams

OVEN TEMPERATURE CONVERSIONS

Degrees Fahrenheit	Degrees Celsius
200 degrees F	95 degrees C
250 degrees F	120 degrees C
275 degrees F	135 degrees C
300 degrees F	150 degrees C
325 degrees F	160 degrees C
350 degrees F	180 degrees C
375 degrees F	190 degrees C
400 degrees F	205 degrees C
425 degrees F	220 degrees C
450 degrees F	230 degrees C

BAKING PAN SIZES

U.S.	Metric
8 × 1½ inch round baking pan	20 × 4 cm cake tin
9 × 1½ inch round baking pan	23 × 3.5 cm cake tin
1 × 7 × 1½ inch baking pan	28 × 18 × 4 cm baking tin
13 × 9 × 2 inch baking pan	30 × 20 × 5 cm baking tin
2 quart rectangular baking dish	30 × 20 × 3 cm baking tin
15 × 10 × 2 inch baking pan	30 × 25 × 2 cm baking tin (Swiss roll tin)
9 inch pie plate	22 × 4 or 23 × 4 cm pie plate
7 or 8 inch springform pan	18 or 20 cm springform or loose bottom cake tin
9 × 5 × 3 inch loaf pan	23 × 13 × 7 cm or 2 lb narrow loaf or pate tin
1½ quart casserole	1.5 liter casserole
2 quart casserole	2 liter casserole

Index